Yours Because of Calvary

The Life and Times of
Apostle Arturo A. Skinner

James C Blocker

To
my Brother
Chris.
God bless you
brother. I pray
this book will be
a blessing as well
as informative

Your Bro.
James Blocker
(Isaiah 3)

Author's Note

"If there's a book that you want to read, but it hasn't been written yet, then you must write it."

—Toni Morrison

Since the death of Arturo Skinner I have been complaining that a book should be written chronicling his life and ministry. Weary of my raving, a friend suggested that I stop "cursing the darkness" and write the book. Admittedly, I procrastinated for years for reasons that are not worth mentioning.

On several occasions I attempted to write, just to abandon the project a short time later. Sometime afterward I visited Washington D.C. to do some research on another project. There I was confronted by a Bishop I was visiting. Pointing his finger at me and with an assertive voice he stated, "This book [on Arturo Skinner] needs to be written, and you are the man to write it!"

I had been told this by several people before and was inspired to write, but after leaving their presence the inspiration died. However, this time the feeling persisted. The result is the book, *Yours Because of Calvary: The Life and Times of Apostle Arturo A. Skinner.*

As the title purports, this book is not limited to Apostle Skinner, but includes some of the events that defined the times in which his ministry flourished. The scope of this book primarily deals with where Pastor Skinner is appropriated in Pentecostal history from the late 1950s to 1975.

I was challenged by some persons who asked "Why are you

writing this book on Arturo Skinner?" I am going to accept the challenge and answer their inquiry.

History Demands it

First and foremost history demands it. Part of the focus of this book is the church as it is informed by Black Pentecostalism. And in Black Pentecostalism, Pastor Skinner is an essential figure in what is known as the "Deliverance Movement." In order for one to have a more complete historical record there must be a reliable, documented account on those persons who helped shape the movement. Otherwise the contributions and legacies of pioneers, along with their memory, will fade into obscurity.

Setting the Record Straight

There is also the need to set the record straight. I have discovered, in a few of the history books that mention Pastor Skinner, some misinformation in reference to him. These authors, albeit well-meaning, have misstated many of the facts.

For example, one historian has Pastor Skinner's ministry being established in the late 1940s. However his conversion was not until the early 1950s. Another historian has him dying at sixty-one years of age. The fact, however, is that he died at age fifty. These are just two examples of misinformation written in reference to Arturo Skinner.

Why Now?

Another question that was posed to me is, "Why, thirty-seven years after his death, are you writing a book on Arturo Skinner?" My response is very brief and simple. Procrastination aside, I will reply with another question "If not now, when?"

To the many who lived during the times spoken of in this work and that knew Arturo Skinner personally, my prayer is that this book brings back pleasant memories.

For those of you who are the "grandchildren" of Deliverance, my hope is that this book will help enlighten you so that you may appreciate, connect with, and identify with your spiritual heritage.

I, along with other former members of Pastor Skinner's church, have been approached by educators and students of Pentecostal history, entreating us to give them some information on Arturo Skinner. I trust this tome will at least serve as a source that will assist future generations in their research.

Dedication

This book is dedicated to all of the unsung heroes of Deliverance. Those people who sacrificed time, talent, and treasure for the sake of the ministry. The "prayer warriors" who prayed consistently for the ministry, many times forgoing rest. To the givers, who gave sacrificially even though it was inconvenient, and to the workers, who worked faithfully, often receiving little recognition.

Acknowledgements

I would like to thank all of those that helped with the development of this work. If it were not for them this book would not have been possible.

First, I want to thank Rev. Elizabeth Ray for arranging a formal introduction to Apostle Skinner.

I want to also thank all of the sons and daughters of Deliverance, whom over the years have shared their personal stories with me of Apostle Skinner. At the time I had no idea it would result in the creation of this book.

I want to also acknowledge the late Lelia Lockwood for her book on Arturo Skinner entitled, *When I Met the Master*, (© 1976, Park Pub. Co. publisher) which laid some of the groundwork for this book.

Additional thanks to:

Bishop Roderick R. Caesar Jr., Bishop James H. Everett Jr., Apostle Richard D. Henton, Barbara Moose-Jacobs, Bishop Matthew Johnson, Bishop Wayne L. Johnson, Alfred (Butch) Simmons, and Dennis Tucker.

Thanks to my Philadelphia connection for sharing their information:

Pastors John Blaine and Timothy Jones, and Bishop Franklin McCloud.

Special thanks to:

Bishop Peter and Pastor Myrna Hallenbeck for their interviews, and for freely sharing with me their archive of past issues of the *Deliverance Voice* and other historical documents.

Rev. Allen Green (Skinner) for reconnecting me to past Deliverance members, sharing his unique insights, and the many hours he and I spent on the phone discussing this work.

To Joyce Holmes, Elaine Jacobs, Dr. Shayne Lee, Betty Holmes-Memminger,* Bishop Alfred Owens and Henry and Effie Soles; for their encouragement and invaluable suggestions.

To Rev. Elaine Lee: No one "translates" *Blockereze* into English as well as her. Thank you my sister for the use of your editing skills.

To my lovely wife Wandra for her suggestions and for listening to me read each chapter *ad infinitum*. Thank you for your patience. Love you sweetheart.

To our offspring Tamara, Tanya, and James II, thank you for listening and adding your critique of this work.

And not to be forgotten, our *second generation of love*, Jamar and Denir. Also our son-in-law, Savage Walker.

*deceased

Commendations

"Arturo Skinner was the 'father' of Deliverance" Bishop Gilbert E. Patterson Presiding Bishop COGIC (2000-2007)

"Pastor Blocker took me back, to the behind the scenes ministry and life of an anointed minister... The names of co-workers in the ministry, and details of events brought back the joys of having served on a team focused on spreading the gospel..."

Bishop James H Everett Jr. Presiding Bishop Deliverance Jesus is Coming

This composition by Rev. James Blocker depicts an authentic, thorough, and accurate account of the life and legacy of the late Apostle Arturo Skinner and the organization, growth, and development of the Deliverance Movement. The author has done an impeccable job in his research and writings providing a plethora of information about this 20th Century giant and the affect his ministry has had on multitudes throughout Christendom.

This treatise is a masterpiece on the Deliverance Movement segment of church history and should be in every preacher's library and shared with all parishioners.

Bishop Wayne L. Johnson BS MA M.Div., Writer and Historian

Table of Contents

Introduction

It was the decade of the 1960s in America: an era appropriately dubbed, "The Turbulent Sixties." People of the inner cities, especially those of color, were fed up with being disenfranchised and suffering the injustices imposed upon them by the powers that be. Many vented their frustrations through rioting in the streets of Newark, New Jersey; Watts, California; Detroit, Michigan; and New York City, New York. In the South, the Civil Rights Movement led by Dr. Martin Luther King, Jr. was in full bloom. However, in the North the Nation of Islam had come into prominence among young African-American inner-city youth proclaiming Christianity as the "white man's religion." The black revolutionary rallying cry, "Black Power" reverberated upon the lips of many angry inner-city youths as they raised their fists in defiance of the white power structure.

Along with this, many of the youth in the church were beginning to question the relevancy of the African American church and hence the relevancy of the Christian message as proclaimed by the African American preacher.

It was in this milieu that an African American Pentecostal church located in the heart of the inner-cities of Bedford-Stuyvesant in Brooklyn, New York and Newark, New Jersey was experiencing an increase in youth attendance. "Gangbangers," both male and female, were abandoning their delinquent behavior and even reconciling with rival gang members. They devoted their Saturdays, along with their former nemesis, to attend the Brooklyn Deliverance

Evangelistic Center on DeKalb Avenue. The same phenomenon was repeated every Sunday at the Newark Deliverance Evangelistic Center on Central Avenue. Prior to the "mega-church era," the membership of these churches was approximately ten thousand people, with more than fifty percent of the member being twenty-five years old and younger.

Also, without a men's ministry *per se*, the male population was about thirty percent of the church's congregation. The choir totaled close to five-hundred voices and sang on Saturdays and Sundays. When one entered the Brooklyn Center's auditorium, what was conspicuous were the two nine-foot oil paintings of Jesus on both sides of the front of the church. What was so striking about these paintings was that they depicted Jesus as an African American. During the early sixties a painting of a black Jesus was rare to nonexistent in black church sanctuaries.

Inevitably, the questions arose, with so many conflicting voices in the inner city, what or who inspired these youths to commit their Saturdays and Sundays to go to church? Why did these youths stop carrying weapons and start carrying, "The Word?" Why was there such a company of men in this church, when traditionally in African American churches men were scarce?

Every so often a man or woman appears on the canvas of time and makes a lasting influence on humankind. What distinguishes these persons is their vision; they see what others do not see. They are people of faith and they dare to do exploits that others would not. They attract the respect of some and the indignation of others of their contemporaries. They are people of purpose and great passion. They are people of decision, intimidating those who settle for mediocrity and inspiring those who aspire to excellence. They persevere in the face of hardships and difficulties with a determination to finish their assignments. These persons are frequently misunderstood, their confidence oftentimes being mistaken for arrogance.

Arturo Skinner (a.k.a. Apostle Skinner), the pastor of the Brooklyn and Newark Deliverance Evangelistic Centers, was one such man. As in the African tradition which honors and gives reverence to its ancestors, so with this book I honor this "Pentecostal General." Noted by many of his peers as a man ahead of his time, he has set standards that would influence others long after his death.

I first came upon Arturo Skinner when I was thirteen years old, in the winter of 1963 at an evangelistic crusade at the Polish Hall auditorium in Jamaica, New York. I accompanied my grandmother to the crusade, which was hosted by a local pastor, Rev. Moses Taylor. Apostle Skinner was the invited guest preacher that Monday night.

What first impressed me when I entered the building was this very large choir that seemed to me to number in the hundreds. The choir was filled with people whose ages ranged from about thirteen years old to adult. As the choir director positioned himself on the stage, the music started to play and his arms began waving in a deliberate motion as he started to conduct. The choir responded to every movement of the director, evidenced by the synchronized cadences proceeding from the voices of this large assembly of singers. After the song ended, the music continued to play in an upbeat tempo. Many of the people in the choir began thanking God aloud as they raised their hands in submission to the "Spirit." Others, with all of their youthful energy, danced in the aisles, their feet moving in rhythm of the tambourines, the piano, and the "double time" hand-clapping of the audience. I had never seen young people so involved in a church service before. I attended church, but it was not like this. This was my introduction to Pentecostalism or the "Sanctified Church," as it was known to me at the time.

Apostle Skinner came onto the stage to minister, and I was compelled to go forward and give my life to Christ that night. What amazed me, though, was his apparent healing gift. Not only did those persons he prayed for that night testify that they were healed after he prayed for them, but many of them he chose from among those that came forward for salvation, revealing their particular predicament without them telling him. I was so in awe with what transpired that night that I told many of my friends the next day what I had witnessed. They came to the crusade with me the following night, but Apostle Skinner was only scheduled to preach for one night. However, our paths would converge again and he would become my mentor and "spiritual father."

Just as with any man or woman, including biblical characters, they all possess human imperfections. With that in mind, I will state the objective of this work, which is not to deify Arturo Skinner, neither is it an exposé magnifying his shortcomings. It is, however, an honest and balanced look at a man of God whose life and ministry testifies to the grace of God in one's life regardless of one's flaws.

CHAPTER ONE

The Call

Before I formed you in the womb I knew you, before you were born I set you apart....

(Jeremiah 1:5 NIV)

It was a balmy sixty degrees on a Tuesday evening, the twenty-fifth of March, six o'clock Post Meridian in the year of our Lord, nineteen hundred and seventy-five, that the Deliverance Temple located at 621 Clinton Avenue in Newark, New Jersey was host to thousands of mourners. Both ministers and laypersons from across the nation and around the world gathered to pay homage to the memory of Arturo Skinner.

Arturo Skinner was a man acknowledged by many as the "Father of Deliverance." Numerous people made financial sacrifices to attend this historic event. Accolades such as, "There will never be another one like him," or, "The church has lost a general," and, "He was a man ahead of his time..." were heard amongst the multitude of mourners in attendance. Tributes poured in from across the nation, including persons of all stations in life, politicians, business people, religious leaders, and even those people marginalized by society whose lives he had touched.

Many who could not enter the building because of the masses, spilled out onto the street with throngs of mourners claiming him as their spiritual father. Pastors and other ministers were testifying that he was their inspiration and had aided them in their ministries. Many others were bearing witness to his apparent "healing gift," proclaiming that they were cured of various illnesses through the laying on of hands. Others accredited their careers and college education to his philanthropy and guidance.

Inside the church, the nearly five-hundred-voice choir began marching in singing what had become a familiar refrain to those who have attended past funerals at the Deliverance Temple:

"How I got ohh-ver, how I got over my Lord, my-y soul, looks, back, an-nd won-ders, won-ders, won-ders—how I got ohh-ver."

Upbeat gospel songs usually used when the church was rejoicing, accompanied the Pentecostal funeral, referred to as a "home-going." However, in the midst of the jubilation, as to be expected, many in attendance were quietly weeping. Meanwhile others were still misty-eyed, braving out the moment attempting to hold back their tears. One could only imagine what was going through Rev. Ray S. Blake's mind as he prepared himself to present the eulogy of such a renowned figure. Many in attendance were welling up with tears, perhaps reminiscing on something he said or did that changed their lives. Others, perplexed and dismayed, pondered, "Why was he taken from us so soon?" and "What is going to happen now?" For the "spiritual" sons and daughters it was as though a parent had died. To others he was as a close relative or perhaps a dear friend. To many, he was a mentor who deceased before concluding his or her training, leaving the student with a feeling of abandonment and wondering if there was some final lesson that he most wanted to convey before departing this life.

Arturo Skinner (a.k.a. Apostle Skinner) had, after only twenty years in ministry, built a world-wide organization that far exceeded many ministries in existence twice as long. At the time of his death, according to *The Amsterdam News*, Skinner had, "Built [his ministry] to over 100 evangelistic centers in principal cities in the United States and several foreign missions…"

Celebrated for miraculous healings that accompanied his ministry reveals only a minute portion of his life.

Arturo A. Skinner was born Arthur Alfred Skinner in Brooklyn, New York on December 15, 1924 to Ethel Rhoda and James Leon Skinner, Sr. Born of West Indian descent, Arthur had two older brothers, James Jr. (Bucky) and Clyde and one younger brother, Kenneth.

During Arthur's formative years, the family did not have an easy time of it. The Skinner family lived on the seventeen-hundred block in Brooklyn on Fulton Street, a flat not suitable for four boys and their parents. The winters were especially harsh for the Skinners because the apartment was cold; half of it had to be closed off at night so that the stove could heat the room.

Skinner always spoke affectionately of his mother. Ethel Rhoda was a woman small in stature, about four feet eleven inches, and had only the equivalent of a third grade education. However, despite her petite frame she was strong-willed in her discipline. She was also a devoted Christian and a member of the Church of the Nazarene, a holiness church. In his "testimonial sermon" entitled, *When I Met the Master*, Skinner also spoke fondly of his mother's church, stating:

"They hugged and kissed one another there was such love on board. You could feel it going from heart-to-heart and from breast-to-breast. They believed in holy living."

Leila Lockwood, a personal secretary to Skinner, authored a book about him in 1976 entitled, *When I Met the Master,* (not to be confused with the sermon of the same title). She writes that Skinner's father, James, Sr., was thrown out of work and found it impossible to find work because of the Depression. Therefore, his only solution was to return to his native Barbados and try to find employment there.

According to Lockwood, in 1932 James took Arthur and Kenneth to live in Barbados with him. After about a year and a half, James sent the boys back to Brooklyn because he was worried about them being away from their mother so long. That was the last time young Arthur saw his father. James died in Barbados in 1945 at the age of fifty-seven, after a back injury that led to other complications.

The only time I have ever heard Skinner mention his father was in his sermon, "When I Met the Master" and I quote: "My father had gone to the West Indies and left my mother here by herself. There was no man in the house so I took it upon myself to act like a man, while still a little boy."

To help make ends meet, young Arthur took on several menial jobs, one in a local Jewish barbershop cleaning and shining shoes and another job in a poultry store. At a young age, Arthur demonstrated some natural intelligence as he learned to speak Yiddish and Hebrew that he picked up from those in his community. This served him well.

At thirteen, he worked in the borough's Welfare Department, translating for those who spoke only Hebrew and Yiddish.

"At the age of ten, because of his flamboyance even as a child, the predominately Jewish community in which Arthur lived tagged him 'Arturo'" (Lockwood 1976). The new name caught on. Afterward, he legally changed his name to Arturo.

As a child, some people labeled him a preacher because he would often preach around the house, imitating preachers he had heard on the radio, on the street, or at his mother's church.

Arturo also exhibited talent for dancing; being up on all the latest ballroom dances and with a natural ability to tap dance. He knew the latest tunes. Arturo often danced in the street for coins. Economic times were hard for the Skinners, so he dropped out of school in the eighth grade to help with the finances at home. He found work as a shipping clerk, while all the time in the back of his mind he wanted to be a Broadway star. Says Skinner, "Then I started growing up, I wanted my name burning in lights on Broadway, because it kind of looked good to me…."

His break came when some of his friends wanted to introduce him to Joey Adams', talent scout.

"The talent scout, eager for new black talent suggested that they all go over to the Lowes Pitkin, a theater noted for amateur night and vaudeville. The agent was impressed so much that he arranged for Arturo to meet Joey Adams himself." (Lockwood 1976)

In Harlem at the Bowman Café, the Rainbow Room is where Arturo Young (his stage name) was to perform. This venue was a good launching pad for new acts, which could lead to engagements at other clubs.

Arturo was in his element as he began meeting those in the show business world, dancing in nightclubs and even appearing in several Broadway musicals. He even became a choreographer for a time as he developed his unique dancing style. Skinner was a flashy dresser, changing outfits three times a day and on occasion even sporting a turban. As expected, like many other entertainers, Arturo fell into the trappings of the decadent "fast life."

"By the age of twelve years old, I was dancing in night clubs. By the age of fifteen, I was singing in the theaters. By the age of twenty I was an M.C. and promoting my own shows, and at twenty-seven, I had become an alcoholic. I went from drinking whiskey to taking dope."

According to Skinner, at that point in his life he did not want anyone to tell him about God, describing himself as a "God-hater." Even his mother's constant prayers for his salvation caused him much anguish, says Skinner:

"Every time I'd go home my mother would be in her bedroom crying out 'Oh Lord, stretch out your hand…and save Arturo.' I'd stomp through the house [and] I'd start talking 'With all the other sons she's got every time that woman falls on her knees she'd call my name before God.'"

Skinner has admitted to treating his make-up artist and other show business subordinates with contempt, speaking condescendingly to them. His overblown ego, however, deflated when the harsh realities of show business dashed his dreams of becoming a renowned Broadway star. As with many hopefuls with star-struck eyes, Arturo Young was no longer a sought after commodity and engagements became increasingly harder to come by.

In addition, Arturo's overindulgence of alcohol and drug addiction repeatedly resulted in "lost weekends." Regularly, after a weekend of debauchery, his friends would find him lying in the street and would take him home so that he could recuperate. Two members of the church that were close to Skinner, stated in an interview that he pointed out to them one of the places where he used to lay in the gutter where his friends would find him and take him home.

Besides being an alcoholic and a drug abuser, Skinner also had a condition in his head that gave him such excruciating pain that at times he could not even wear a hat.

Death of Ethel Rhoda Skinner

"In 1952 during the Labor Day weekend, Arturo was preparing for a weekend of partying which no doubt included drinking and drugs. After he left his home, eight hours later the call came to Arturo that his mother had a cerebral stroke. He rushed back to Brooklyn to his mother's bedside. Ethel Rhoda laid three days in the hospital unable to communicate, and then she died. She was sixty-one." (Lockwood 1976)

Understandably, Arturo was depressed and inconsolable because of the death of his mother. Adding to the painful loss of his mother was his deteriorating career, his addiction to drugs and his overindulgence of alcohol. Feeling dejected and desperate and believing that he could sink no lower, a few months after his mother died, at the age of only twenty-eight, he decided to take his own life by jumping in front of a moving subway train. He reasoned that if he killed himself, he would rejoin his mother [sic].

In the middle of Atlantic and Rochester Avenues, about three blocks away from the train station, Arturo's faith returned to him.

According to the Deliverance Seventh Anniversary Journal:

"On the way [to commit suicide] on one of the busiest streets of Brooklyn, NY he was stopped by the sound of a commanding voice, 'Arturo, Arturo,' the voice of God called. Turning in amazement, he listened intently as the voice continued: "If you accept me as your personal savior, I will save you, deliver you, and anoint you to preach the gospel." As the voice drifted away, Brother Skinner was held spellbound by the appearance of a vision of what seemed to be a thousand member choir, dressed in flowing robes of blue and gold, chanting the praises of the Lord."

However, in Skinner's own words recorded in his autobiographical sketch, in a later church journal it states:

"Arturo, if you but turn around, I'll save your soul, heal your body, and give you a Deliverance Ministry. I had never heard the term 'Deliverance Ministry.' Yet God told me this was to be my new life."

According to Skinner, God held back the traffic on both sides of the street on this busy thoroughfare. Subsequent to hearing the voice, he asked God to save him. After which he returned to his apartment, called his friends, and began giving away his clothing along with his custom-made furniture. His friends lamented, "Poor Arturo," as they carted away his belongings. Skinner rationalized that those material things were obtained in his "old life"; now he was starting a "new life" and wanted no attachments to the old. Says Skinner, "I gave away all my clothes and all of the things the devil gave me."

In correlation with this in a sermon, Skinner related the account of a bar tab he had incurred before his conversion. Some in the church tried to convince him that he did not have to pay that bill since the tab was acquired while he was still "in the world." However, Arturo, not wanting to leave any loose ends, could not be reconciled with the fact that he owed it. According to Skinner, one night not wanting to be seen by anyone, he slipped behind the tavern and knocked on the back door. The owner came to the door and Skinner paid off his bar tab.

According to Skinner at the time of his "Christ encounter," although he wanted to end his life, he was not financially destitute. "When God saved me I wasn't in the gutter; I had money, stocks and bonds and a beautiful home. I was just getting ready to remodel my home."

After disposing of most of his worldly belongings, with just one suit, one shirt, one coat, his mother's Bible, her Bible commentary, and a suitcase with a few changes of clothes, he journeyed to Connecticut spending fifty-six days and nights, determined to beat his drug addiction "cold turkey." During those tumultuous days, according to Skinner, he fasted and prayed as God dealt with him in dreams and visions. He also took on little odd jobs to sustain himself while contending with his addictions to drugs and alcohol. Convinced he was cured, he returned to New York from his pilgrimage in Connecticut; he was geared up to preach.

When Arturo returned to New York, he did not have much by way of finances. He obtained odd jobs, however it was not enough to sustain him. Olga Smalls, his sister-in-law who was married to his half-brother, Irving, many times came to his aid with money and food.

Arturo got a room on 125th Street in Harlem. There R.C. Lawson, presiding bishop of the Church of Our Lord Jesus Christ, and Louise Prescod would help him on occasions. In addition, his good friend Ohanio Williams often slipped a few dollars under his door to help his friend.

Lockwood reported: "Mother Emma Futch, whom Arturo met in a restaurant on 125th Street, would sometimes buy him a bowl of soup and bread to fill-up on. Though she herself was on welfare, and sometimes had to use credit at the restaurant and pay for the food later, she could not deny Arturo with whom she became very good friends."

Arturo also sought counsel from his late mother's pastor. When Arturo made the pastor aware of his conversion and his eagerness to preach, the pastor informed Arturo that God does not want uneducated preachers and then walked away. Undaunted by the pastor's lack of enthusiasm for his new found passion, Skinner thought to himself that he was going to get educated.

Bethel Bible Institute

During the 1950s, few Pentecostal ministers attended seminary. Pentecostals, for the most part, discouraged their ministers from attending seminary. Most Pentecostals believed that seminaries were too liberal and would be in opposition to the Pentecostal distinctive. Therefore, some Pentecostal churches developed their own schools of the Bible called Bible Institutes, which aligned more with the Pentecostal point of view.

One of those Bible Institutes was the Bethel Bible Institute (B.B.I.), which is located in Jamaica, New York and offered a systematic study of the Bible. This proved to be the solution for many Pentecostals that desired a deeper study of the Bible than the average Bible study, and still stay true to their Pentecostal sensibilities. Dr. Roderick R. Caesar Sr., an erudite and eloquent Bible teacher, was its president.

Caesar was a "classical" Pentecostal. Classical Pentecostal teaching encompasses glossolalia or speaking in tongues, the Trinity, salvation by faith, which includes repentance, the belief and the confession of the Lordship of Jesus and His resurrection being sufficient for one to become "born-again," i. e. saved from his or her sins. In addition, Pentecostals believe in living a "sanctified life" by abstaining from smoking, drinking alcohol, gambling, and other such "worldly" activities, also referring to themselves as "saints" (i.e. God's holy people).

B.B.I. attracted many laypersons and ministers. Among them were Arturo Skinner, who not only studied under Caesar, but also became a member of the Bethel Gospel Tabernacle, the church which Caesar pastored. Without question, Caesar shaped a great deal of Arturo's theology.

Bethel was a part of the United Pentecostal Council of the Assemblies of God, which later licensed Arturo to preach. This is not to be confused with the Assemblies of God, a predominately-white Pentecostal organization.

While attending B.B.I, Skinner began a quest for places where he could satisfy his eagerness to preach. He began by seeking out well-known tent preachers, and he preached in various venues.

According to Skinner, one of those preaching venues was in a tent in which the minister conducting the tent meeting had less than honorable intentions. Observing Skinner's ability to attract people he suggested to Skinner that he could "cash in" on the gullibility of people by selling "blessed candles" and other trinkets to the unsuspecting audience. He also related to Skinner the benefits that would accompany such actions, as a Cadillac car and other material items. That experience was a rude awakening for Arturo, shaking him from his naïveté. He came to the realization that not all preachers were what they claimed to be. According to Skinner after that incident, he vowed never to take God's money or His glory for himself.

Skinner continued to preach at various other locations. While in a Bible class Caesar instructed the class that they needed to be Spirit-filled in order to be effective for God, says Skinner:

"Dr. Caesar, my father in the gospel, said we are not fully capable of doing a work for God until we are filled with the Holy Ghost. Every night after service, I would be at somebody's altar. My [appointment] book was filled with meetings before I had the Holy Ghost; they were always trying to get me to preach everywhere. I told God that I was not going to tell nobody about Him anymore...until He filled me."

At least one of those altars was at a "Oneness" (a.k.a. Jesus Only or Apostolic), Pentecostal church. The Oneness Pentecostals differ from classical Pentecostals in that Oneness Pentecostals do not subscribe to Trinitarian theology. Oneness Pentecostals believe in the *One* "Person" of God (i.e. Jesus is the Father, the Son, and the Holy Spirit) as opposed to the *one* God existing in *three* "Persons." In addition, they affirm that one must be baptized in the name of Jesus and speak with other tongues before one can be considered saved from his or her sins.

Pentecostals routinely conducted all-night prayer meetings called "tarry services." The church designed the tarry services for those who wanted to be Spirit-filled with the evidence of speaking in tongues. Skinner, one time recalling an experience he had at this Oneness church, said that he would attend the tarry service seeking the filling of the Holy Spirit, however, he as of yet had not spoken in tongues. Skinner, being an immature Christian, figured in view of the fact that this church did not consider him saved, there was no point in resisting the temptation to indulge in a cigarette; as mentioned earlier, this was a practice forbidden by Pentecostals.

Nevertheless, both classical and Oneness Pentecostals base much of their spirituality on experiences, and to the Pentecostal there is no greater experience than the filling of the Spirit of God with the evidence of speaking in tongues. The filling with the Spirit meant one had a "power" that they did not possess prior to being filled and now had God's Spirit living in them.

Skinner was passionate about the filling of the Spirit, which consumed him. Skinner made up his mind that he was going to be Spirit-filled. One Friday night there was a tarry service at Bethel. According to Skinner, he was there to be Spirit-filled and was not going to leave until he was filled. After many hours of prayer, all of the other "seekers" gave up and went home. The only ones that remained were Skinner and Caesar.

Skinner said, "About fifty people began to tarry, and at about three a.m. there were half a dozen. By five a.m. it was just Pastor Caesar and myself. I could hear the man of God say 'Son, Jesus is all around you.' I kept saying, 'Hallelujah! and Thank you Jesus!'"

Skinner continued to pray. According to Skinner, at first he was kneeling down, then he laid down. He got tired of that position, so he sat and then stood. Skinner, describing his experience, said it was as rain, with the water first at his feet, then his knees and eventually it reached his tongue and he began to speak in tongues. By that time, it was early in the morning and the sun was coming up. However, Arturo was not tired or sleepy even though he had not slept all night.

After his "Upper Room" experience, while still in B.B.I, Skinner asserted that God would deal with him about his hands. According to Skinner, God said that He was going to use Skinner's hands to open the eyes of the blind, cause cancer to dissolve, and cause tumors to leave bodies.

Says Skinner, "All of the students used to laugh and make fun of my hands. God is going to use these hands for the tearing down of the strongholds of Satan and for the building up of the kingdom of God."

According to Bishop Roderick Caesar, Jr., Skinner was a very active lay leader and spent much of his time working with those at the altar. He also became a popular preacher and had a great impact on the audience. The audience always received his ministry well at Bethel. His relationship to his pastor, according to Caesar, was a devoted, close confidant, along with that of a mentor-mentee bond. When Arturo started his church, the elder Caesar came on a few occasions to preach and encourage his young protégé.

The respect that Skinner had for his mentor lasted throughout his life. The respect appeared to be shared as on one occasion Rev. T.B. Jackson, a former pastor in Deliverance, asked Caesar to officiate the service on his elevation to the office of Bishop. Caesar was aware that Skinner was acquainted with Jackson, so he sought Skinner's recommendation as to the character of Jackson.

In 1997, B.B.I. posthumously awarded the *Outstanding Student Award* to Rev. Arturo Skinner for outstanding Christian Service to the body of Christ. At the time, I was a part of the faculty of B.B.I. and was asked by the administration of B.B.I. to receive the award on Skinner's behalf.

The Watsons

Arturo struggled to keep himself afloat during this lean period of his life. It is not certain why, but he turned to his friend Katie Hicks for help when he needed a place to stay. Hicks called her dear friend, Violet Watson, and, according to Lockwood, "Pleaded with her to take Arturo into her home." Watson lived in a sixteen-room brownstone at 117 West 120th Street. A widow, she opened her home to young women.

"By all logic… Watson should have said, 'No' first off… Mrs. Watson generally charged seven dollars a week for rooms. Here was a pathetic looking soul who could not pay a cent. Mrs. Watson knew it made no sense, but she said, 'Yes' and Arturo moved in." (Lockwood, 1976)

Arturo had no money to pay his rent so he bartered by doing the many house chores that needed doing. The relationship between Arturo and Watson developed into a mother-son relationship. Arturo also developed a close sister and brother relationship with her two daughters Barbara and Grace along with close bonds with James Watson, Jr., her son, who was a Justice of the United States Customs Court. His close association with the Watsons became a very useful connection to Skinner and his ministry.

Arturo graduated from B.B.I. (circa. 1954) and was to be ordained an evangelist on Palm Sunday (circa. 1955). Around the time for him to be ordained, James Watson asked him, "Brother what are you going to wear to be ordained in?" James knew that Arturo had nothing suitable to wear for his ordination. Therefore, he took Arturo to Wallach's clothing store and bought him a new suit and shoes.

Brother Skinner was now Evangelist Skinner and he wasted no time in holding evangelistic meetings in and about the surrounding area.

Dr. Roderick R. Caesar Sr.

Brooklyn Center

Apostle Consecration

CHAPTER TWO

God Wants to Heal You

We are so involved and preoccupied with the modernistic approach to the Gospel, that we have by-passed the obvious, a life yielded to God.

Arturo Skinner, "9 Gifts of the Spirit"

Virtually every Pentecostal organization traces its roots, in regard to speaking in tongues, either directly or indirectly to the Azusa St. Revival of 1906, in which an African American minister, Bishop William Joseph Seymour was the catalyst and pastor. (Seymour was posthumously conferred the title "Bishop" at the 100th anniversary of the Azusa St. Revival in Los Angeles, California 2006 by Bishop Charles Blake, C.O.G.I.C. et.al.)

According to David E. Harrell in his book, *All Things Are Possible,* among Pentecostals the period of 1947 to 1958 was known as the "healing revival" (Harrell 1978). During the 1950s the healing revival took on the label "Deliverance." Some of the healing/deliverance evangelists of this era were afforded widespread publicity thanks in part to the publication of Gordon Lindsay's magazine "Voice of Healing" (V.O.H.). However, the V.O.H., for the most part, highlighted the popular white healing evangelists. There were also black evangelists and pastors that built their ministries emphasizing healing before and during the so-called healing revival. *The Encyclopedia of African American Religions* lists a few of them, such as, Charles Price Jones, Charles H. Mason and W.H.

Fulford, were known for healing ministries. During the early 20th century there were African American women that were also known for healing ministries namely: Rosa Artemus Horn in Harlem, in Chicago, Mattie B. Pool of the Bethlehem Healing Temple and Lucy Smith also from Chicago.

Even so, post W.W. II, white evangelists as William Branham, Jack Coe, and Oral Roberts among others, were some of the biggest names of the healing evangelists and controlled the tent circuit. According to Skinner, he asked God, why were there no black ministers of that caliber with a deliverance ministry. Skinner maintained that God spoke to him and said if a black man would pay the price, then He would use him. According to Skinner, he vowed that he would be one black man that would "pay the price." Paying the price, according to Skinner, amounted to spending long hours in prayer, fasting, and living an exemplary and "separated" life.

"In general Pentecostals believed deliverance from physical sickness is provided for in the atonement and is the privilege of all believers Jesus' death purchased healing for both soul and body" (Harrell, 1978). Scriptures such as Exodus 15:26 which reads "I am the Lord that heals you," Isaiah 53:5 "But he was wounded for our transgressions he was bruised for our iniquities…and *with his stripes we are healed*." (emphasis mine). In addition, James 5:15 "And the prayer of faith shall save the sick and the Lord will raise him up." A myriad of other scriptures were used as proof texts for guaranteed healing. Harrell also notes in his work "The crucial condition for the receiving of divine healing was an appropriate faith." (Harrell, 1978)

In the early days of his ministry, Skinner attended the crusades of healing evangelists A. A. Allen and Oral Roberts, among others. He usually sat in the back, observing what was going on. On one of those visits to an Oral Roberts tent meeting, Arturo experienced what would become a hallmark in his own ministry; that being a divine healing. As mentioned earlier, Skinner had migraine headaches so severe that at times he could not even wear a hat. Prior to the start of the service, Skinner stuck his head through a flap in the tent and experienced what he described as "feeling something fall on his head." According to Skinner he was healed instantaneously and never suffered from those headaches again.

It is reasonable to assume that he took pointers and may have even adopted many of the techniques of some of the tent evangelists. Arturo boasted that he had an extensive library on the deliverance ministry. The healing evangelists or others involved with the healing revival were the authors of these "deliverance books."

Several of the prevailing viewpoints of the healing revivalists influenced Arturo. In his work, "God Wants to Heal You," Skinner proclaimed that it is *always* God's will to heal and that sickness is of the devil, but cautioned that if one does not have the faith to be healed, then one should seek the aid of a good doctor.

In his book, *9 Gifts of the Spirit*, (published posthumously), Skinner states, "The Gift of healing is a supernatural performance through the working of the Holy Ghost... The art of divine healing is the creating of that which was not or recreating of that which was destroyed. It is life ['s] triumph over death" (Skinner, 1975). This is not to say that we will never die, but according to Skinner, God's best is for the Christian to live in "divine health" pending death.

Ironically, Skinner objected to the label "faith healer," because he contended that the title "faith healer" put too much emphasis upon faith. I have heard him state on a number of occasions that "faith is not the healer, God is; faith is only the 'train' that delivers the healing."

It is, nonetheless, completely understandable that with the testimonies of healing throughout his ministry, that he would be convinced that he had ample evidence for believing in divine healing. In addition, it was through these reported healings that crowds were attracted to his church and crusades.

Prior to the emergence of Skinner's healing ministry, those in New Jersey in search of a healing ministry, for the most part, sought it in the healing crusades services of famed healing evangelists A.A. Allen, Jack Coe, and Oral Roberts. Arturo Skinner's healing ministry began in the early to mid-1950s, and continued until his death in 1975.

The Birth of Deliverance Evangelistic Center

In September of 1956, a Polish woman, Mary Amartys, began conducting prayer meetings in her home in Newark, New Jersey. Amartys invited Skinner to come and pray. Those that attended the prayer meetings began experiencing healing from various illnesses. According to a person close to these events, the word began to spread among church circles that a black man was praying for the sick and receiving miraculous results just like Oral Roberts.

Amartys in the first Deliverance Women's Day Service journal, recalled those days:

"God laid the burden of souls upon my heart. My home was opened for prayer meetings, and I invited the people who wanted to pray with me for the souls of men. I invited Bro. Skinner to come in and pray with us. God manifested His power; the sick were healed and delivered."

Amartys also invited Rev. Thorton, a local pastor, and his wife to the prayer services. Thorton was so impressed with Skinner's ministry that he invited him to conduct a revival at his church on Peshine Ave. in Newark.

In two weeks' time his place became too small so they rented the Essex Theater on Springfield Ave. After that the meeting moved to the Community Center on High St. in Newark, then the Masonic Temple at 188 Belmont Avenue. For about three years Skinner and his supporters moved from location to location until in 1959 he came upon a theatre at 505 Central Avenue in Newark that seated twelve-hundred persons. This became their home and they named it the Newark Deliverance Evangelistic Center.

Skinner uniquely held his Sunday services at three p.m. claiming that the Lord instructed him to do so. The strategy was that those persons connected with his evangelistic group that were members of other churches, being that most churches started their services at eleven a.m., could attend their own church services and still be present at the Deliverance services. Consequently, a number of members of other churches attended the three p.m. Deliverance services every Sunday.

Along with the services in Newark, New Jersey, he also

conducted healing campaigns in Brooklyn, New York known as "Deliverance Rallies." Skinner's timing for his evangelistic meetings in Brooklyn was impeccable. According to Clarence Taylor in his book, *The Black Churches of Brooklyn*, quoting the *Amsterdam News*, writes "By the 1950s Pentecostal churches were the 'fastest growing churches in Brooklyn.'" (Taylor, 1994).

Skinner was not a part of any major Pentecostal organization. Although the United Pentecostal Council of the Assemblies of God (UPCAG) ordained Skinner under their auspices, with his pastor's blessing, he later left Bethel and U.P.C.A.G., venturing out on his own. Despite being an evangelistic effort and not an organized church, he had a faithful following that traveled with him to the many places he conducted his meetings. Sometime around the late 1950s, Arturo conducted "The Salvation and Healing Caravan." Those with cars were to take as many people as they could to the services. Evangelist Clifford Simmons assisted Skinner; The Faith Gospel Singers were one of the groups that assisted with the music. Skinner received his charter for the Newark Deliverance Evangelistic Center, Inc. on October 1957. After one year of inception, the church had a membership of over four-hundred people. ("First Woman's Day Service Journal").

Because of the masses in attendance at the Deliverance Rallies in Brooklyn, as was the case in Newark, Skinner moved his rallies to various locations. Skinner conducted some of his first campaigns at 182 Gates Ave. (circa. 1958) then 404 Gates Ave. Next he conducted his services at the Bedford Y.M.C.A., each becoming inadequate to accommodate the crowds. After which, he purchased the Old Kismet theatre at 785 DeKalb Ave. (circa. 1962) with a seating capacity of fifteen-hundred, naming it the Brooklyn Deliverance Evangelistic Center (later changing the name to the Brooklyn Deliverance Tabernacle).

The Brooklyn Center afforded Skinner the liberty to expand. Before the Brooklyn Center, the church office was in his apartment. The Brooklyn Center also housed the executive offices, the administration offices, the bookstore, the printing plant, the photography studio, recording studio, auxiliary rooms, and choir room.

In 1958, Skinner started the Hour of Deliverance radio broadcast.

A "Negro" Jesus

When one entered the Brooklyn Deliverance Center for the first time, it became evident that this was not the archetypal black church. In the Brooklyn Deliverance Center, located on both sides of the platform were two nine-foot oil paintings depicting Jesus as a black man. While it is more common today, in the early sixties even among some black churches, a painting of a black Jesus was controversial. One must keep in mind that society referred to African Americans as "Negroes" and "Colored People." The term "black" in reference to one's race was offensive. In addition, African Americans were, by the dominate society, considered inferior to Caucasians many times by inference and other times overtly. Even some churches taught that there was a curse put upon Ham, Noah's black son, and the curse passed to all black people.

Most people, during this time, visualized Jesus as depicted by Leonardo Da Vinci's "Last Supper" painting, which portrays Jesus as having European features, white skin, and hair down to his shoulders. The painting of a "Negro Jesus" with kinky hair was unorthodox and regarded radical.

I once overheard a conversation Skinner was having with another minister concerning the clamor regarding the paintings. Skinner, not offering any apologies or excuses, told this minister that he did not ask the artist to paint a black Jesus, he just asked for two paintings and the artist, Mr. Sapp, interpreted Jesus as black. All the same, the paintings fit perfectly into Skinner's point of view.

Skinner's Influence on African American Pentecostalism

The distinctiveness of Arturo Skinner's healing ministry amongst most other African American healing ministries ultimately caused his ministry to be prominent for his emphasis on "Deliverance." As stated in chapter one, Skinner is reputed as being the "Father of Deliverance." *The Encyclopedia of African American Religions* corroborates this assertion, stating that:

"The deliverance movement among Black Pentecostals emerged from the ministry of Arturo Skinner who expanded the traditional black Pentecostal emphasis on healing to include demonology and exorcism, and heightened the accent on the miraculous."

Many pastors would refer people to Skinner for prayer. As one pastor stated, "I sent all of my 'hard cases' to Pastor Skinner [for deliverance]." "Deliverance," as defined by Skinner, means being set free from all bondages of the mind, body, soul, and circumstance.

Skinner continued having services in Newark on Sundays and in Brooklyn on Saturdays. Every Saturday evening chartered buses left Newark for the eight p.m. Saturday night services at the Brooklyn Deliverance Center. Cars and buses arriving at the Brooklyn Deliverance Center lined DeKalb Avenue, hindering the flow of traffic as members disembarked from the buses and other parishioners from their vehicles.

The female choir members dressed in white blouses and dark skirts. The males in white shirts and dark pants, each and every one donning a red button with the inscription in black lettering that read, "Christ is the Answer."

On Sundays, the identical scene repeated itself in Newark as a sea of choir members and parishioners flooded Central Avenue. Skinner's Sunday services continued to be held at three p.m. The strategy continued to work and the church filled every Sunday with visitors from all over the cities of Newark and New York. For the convenience of those without transportation there were chartered buses leaving every Sunday from Brooklyn and Harlem, New York, going to the Newark Deliverance Center.

By the early 1960s, in both the Brooklyn and Newark services, Skinner was speaking to capacity crowds. In the early 1970s, he changed the time of the Brooklyn Center service to three p.m., which amazingly did not affect the crowd.

Not all of the other Pentecostal pastors, however, received Skinner's success favorably. Concerned with a loss of membership some of the pastors of these churches would discourage their congregants from attending Skinner's meetings. Many times, they had warranted concerns. Several persons that were healed in Skinner's services did not return to their own churches, choosing rather to stay where they experienced "the power."

Vinson Synan, a Pentecostal historian, in his book, *The Century of the Holy Spirit: 100 Years of Pentecostal and Charismatic Renewal*, states:

"During the 1950's, the black Pentecostal movement received its first major internal challenge with the rise of the African-American deliverance movement with its focus on exorcism and miracles... Deliverance ministries were touted as being more in touch with the power of God than the average black Pentecostal congregations." (Synan, 2001)

In addition, in referring to African Americans' influences on the Deliverance movement, Synan writes, "By 1956, Arturo Skinner was a key figure..." Some of the other African American preachers mentioned reputed as possessing a deliverance ministry are, H.W. Goldsberry, of Chicago, Richard Henton, also from Chicago, and E.E. Cleveland, Sr., from Berkeley, California (Synan, 2001).

Skinner continued to expand, conducting crusades in Philadelphia, PA. (circa. 1962) starting at Rev. Robert T. Robertson's church and later moving to the Imperial Ballroom on 60th and Market Street. His crusades were attracting large crowds rivaling that of popular tent evangelist A.A. Allen in attendance. As in Brooklyn, Philadelphia had a strong black Pentecostal presence with Church of God in Christ, Church of the Living God, and Fire Baptized etc. In addition, Thea Jones, a local white pastor with a large African American following, held church services at the historic Metropolitan Opera Theatre (a.k.a. The Met) attracting large crowds.

Around 1963, Skinner purchased the Hamilton Theatre located at 5926 Lansdown Ave., naming it the Pennsylvania Deliverance Center. He appointed Harold Benjamin, a young, charismatic, gifted preacher, and graduate of the prestigious Zion Bible Institute of Rhode Island, as pastor. Occasionally Skinner came down to run healing crusades in Philadelphia in places like the Philadelphia Arena, to help bolster the attendance at the Philadelphia church.

Skinner was renowned for attracting a significant number of youth to the church. Included were members of local street gangs that started attending the church as they renounced their gang life and made a commitment to Christ. One of the factors that made these conversions credible was that those that lived in the community knew many of these delinquents. Some with notorious reputations

started attending the church with their Bibles in hand and even testi-
fied on street corners about their commitment to Christ.

Conspicuous was the relatively large company of men which
joined themselves to his ministry. There were also many people that
transferred their memberships, joining Deliverance from churches
of various mainline denominations and from other Pentecostal
churches. Both classical and Oneness Pentecostals joined the
Deliverance Center. This is significant because classical and Oneness
Pentecostals, although at times shared church services together, bit-
terly disagreed with respect to the nature of God, the qualifications
for one to become a "true" Christian and the baptism formula.

Prayer, Fasting and Anointing

Apostle Richard Henton, a nationally renowned pastor, in an
interview stated that Skinner told him that he (Henton) should
have a "real strong" mid-week service, since he was in demand as
a preacher, which caused him to be away from his church often.
Skinner reasoned that in so doing, Henton could travel during the
rest of week, be back by Sunday and not be away from his members
as often. Skinner, in instructing the pastors would often assert, "You
can't pastor on the road" which is to say, you must be present at
your church to care for the flock. Skinner made a point never to miss
consecutive Sundays away from his church.

Tuesday night was Skinner's strong midweek service known as
"Prayer Fasting and Anointing" and was held at the Newark location. There were between eight-hundred to one-thousand persons in
attendance. Pastors and laypersons from all over the city of Newark
attended the Tuesday services. On Tuesdays, the young people were
in charge of the early prayer, which started at three p.m. At six p.m.,
the adults took over as the young people retired to the dining area
to do their homework. Before Skinner came out to minister, Corrine
Austin, one of the mothers of the church, would teach a Bible lesson.
One of the reasons Tuesday night services were well-attended is that
Skinner would routinely anoint all those in attendance.

What still amazes me is that with the thousands in Deliverance,
Skinner availed himself to meeting almost everyone personally. If

someone wanted to meet him, all one had to do was be in Brooklyn on a Thursday night, a Saturday afternoon or in Newark on Tuesday night before service, which was his counseling sessions, and arrangements would be made to at least meet with him.

The negative aspect, however, was that Skinner was over-extended by the sheer number of people in need of counseling. It kept him close to the people on one hand, but on the other hand perhaps wore on him both physically and mentally. He did all of the counseling because there were not many people that Skinner trusted to counsel the church members. People criticized him as being insecure since he did not trust others to counsel the church members. Others were saying, "He loves those people *too* much" [sic].

Elevation to Apostle

On April 28, 1963, Skinner made a controversial move by laying claim to the office of apostle. Along with Charles Miles of Ecorse, Michigan, Skinner, at the fourth annual Deliverance Convention, was "elevated" to the office of apostle in an elaborate ceremony at the Newark Armory, located in Newark, New Jersey. Four-thousand followers and well-wishers witnessed the ceremony; Rev. A. L. Alaman being the chief consecrator.

The basis for the controversy was that apostles were *special messengers* chosen by Jesus and along with the prophets, laid the foundation of the church (Eph.2:20). Some in the churches at large held the view that if an individual assumed the title "apostle," that particular person was implying that they were above other ministers and their ministry was more important. In addition, other churches held the belief that the office of apostle phased-out when the last apostle of the first century died.

Skinner was not the first black minister to assume the office of apostle. In 1907, the Church of God in Christ elected Charles H Mason "Chief Apostle" of the church. However, he was renowned as "Bishop Mason." Conversely, Skinner, while known as Pastor or Evangelist Skinner was even more renowned as Apostle Skinner. Although Skinner was not the first contemporary minister to adopt the title apostle, he made it very visible and took the brunt of the criticism for being presumptuous enough as to assume such an office.

A number of people not willing to recognize Arturo Skinner as an apostle, would refer to him as just "Skinner," while referring to their own pastors accompanied with a title. Within the black church, it is a sign of disrespect to address the minister just by his or her first or last name without accompanying it with a title.

The Deliverance church responded by defending the present-day office of the apostle, basing their belief on Ephesians 4:11-13 which lists the apostle among the titles of prophet, evangelist, pastor, and teacher [v11]. According to the text, God called all of the "ministry offices" to "mature the saints for the work of ministry..." [v12]. "Until we all come to the unity of the faith..." [v13]. The rationale is that if the other ministries exist in modern times to "mature the saints" so then does the apostle. Furthermore, since the church has not, as of yet, come to the "unity of the faith" then the ministry of the apostle is still pertinent. Currently the title "apostle" is more widely accepted in Pentecostal and charismatic circles.

Deliverance was set up with Skinner as the "Chief Apostle." There were other apostles, as mentioned earlier, Charles Miles, of Ecorse, Michigan. In addition, there was Leroy Battle from Minneapolis, Minn. and later on, R.C. Duke from Trinidad, West Indies. Skinner's church was the largest in the fellowship, with churches concentrated on the eastern coast of the United States. He often stated that the Deliverance fellowship was not an organization, but an "organism."

Because of his reputation for being generous, many independent churches wanted to join themselves to Deliverance. Skinner did not allow every church to come into the Deliverance fellowship. I overheard a conversation Skinner was having with one of his ministers while we were overseas. I heard him tell this minister that he was not going to accept all the churches that wanted to join themselves to Deliverance because he did not want the inevitable isms and schisms that would accompany churches of diverse theological backgrounds.

Skinner's Ministry

Skinner did not specialize in preaching, as with some of the great expositors of that era such as Bishop F.D. Washington, for example. Skinner's ministry focused more on the demonstration of spiritual gifts. Pentecostals not only believe in speaking with other tongues and healing but *all* of the nine gifts of the Spirit as listed in the twelfth chapter of First Corinthians. Skinner, reputed as gifted with many of those spiritual gifts, often held his audiences spellbound as he demonstrated his "spiritual enablement."

Skinner's preaching style was more of a direct approach toward preaching. When he spoke on sin for instance, he called it sin with no qualification. Skinner typically prefaced his sermons by asserting, "I was in my prayer room this week where God has been speaking to me." This statement added to his mystique, lending support to the belief that God spoke with him on a regular basis.

On the surface, Skinner's preaching appeared dogmatic especially when it came to sin. Though he knew sin to be sin, he also understood, as he remarked giving credit to the mothers of the church for teaching him that, "It takes time to live holy." He knew that after conversion one might perhaps still practice some of his or her sinful ways from time-to-time, and yet not lose their salvation. Skinner even admitted that in his early Christian walk he still had a nicotine habit for a time, although he had conquered his drug addiction. While not as rigid in respect to the loss of one's salvation as many Pentecostals of that time, he was not an advocate of the doctrine of "eternal security" or "once saved always saved."

In addition, he thought it more needful for him to give added attention to his prayer life. In an interview with Bishop Matthew Johnson, one of his former drivers, he asserts when he picked Skinner up in the morning for an appointment that he (Skinner) would not say a word to him. Skinner remained silent until a certain time of the day, and then all of a sudden he started talking. Johnson surmised that Skinner was in prayer until a certain time.

On occasion, he would mention his personal prayer life, stating he would often spend all night in prayer. I recall one time we were overseas on a crusade when a local radio personality asked Skinner to be a guest on his program that day. Skinner responded stating that he had to get before the Lord in prayer and would not be available for interviews until the next day. His statement, following his postponement to be a guest on the program, still lingers indelibly in my mind and defined for me his approach toward ministry as he declared; "I have the message, but what I need now is the anointing."

Reach the Lost at Any Cost

As one would imagine, Skinner preached many sermons on God's power to miraculously heal infirmities. However, the significance placed upon divine healing paled in comparison to the importance he placed on attracting new converts. In church vernacular, the more accepted terms are "soul-winning" or "reaching the lost." The winning of souls was the focal point of Skinner's ministry. This is where the influence of his "father" in the gospel and former pastor, Bishop Roderick Caesar, Sr. who had a penchant for soul-winning became apparent. The importance Skinner placed on reaching lost souls was legendary. He often stated if you were not seeking to win lost souls your ministry meant nothing. I have even heard him instruct the singers of the church that if another church invited them to perform a concert and did not allow them to make an altar call, they should not accept the engagement.

All of the lay-members and ministers of the church had this mantra burned into their psyches: "Reach the Lost at Any Cost." However, this was more than a catch-phrase to Skinner; it was his way of life. Skinner would even approach persons in a train station and share the gospel or invite the taxicab driver he was riding with to receive Christ. As well, Skinner was not above having his driver pull the car over to the side while he exited the car to reach out to a drug addict lying on the street. Skinner had a special compassion for drug addicts, perhaps because he was once addicted to drugs and understood their struggles.

With regard to drug abusers, there were many ex-drug offenders in the church. So much so, that Skinner instituted an "ex-drug addicts Sunday." Once a year the ex-drug addicts conducted the entire Sunday service. Skinner also instituted an annual "Backslider's

Sunday." On those Sundays, Skinner made a special appeal to those who left the church and had gone back to their old ways. They were encouraged to return to God, restored spiritually, and then reinstated into the church.

The youth would also get involved with soul-winning. Every Saturday before church service, the "Invaders for Christ" conducted outdoor services in Brooklyn. They were so-named, because they were said to "invade" the devil's territory with witnessing and street service meetings. In addition, on Monday nights the "Forerunners" held street services on the corner of 42nd Street and Eighth Ave. in Manhattan.

A Typical Service

Skinner was a stickler when it came to time; he would not tolerate lateness. The services were to start promptly at the designated time. This was necessary, especially when he conducted crusades at the various auditoriums, because he had to stay within the boundaries of the allotted time. One of the first things Skinner did when he approached the podium was to take off his watch and place it on the podium facing up, as to keep aware of the time. One of his former drivers said that if he was late picking him up, Skinner would leave and when the driver finally arrived, there would be a message left for the driver with information on where to meet him.

Members of the Mothers' Auxiliary always sat in the front rows of the church in every church service in which Skinner was ministering. Their assignment was to pray for him as he ministered to the sick. You would not notice them unless you passed by the front row, then you would see them with their hands stretched out toward Skinner and their voices lifted just above a murmur as they continually offered prayer on his behalf.

After he concluded his sermons, Skinner always made altar calls for those to come forward to receive Christ. Skinner was aware that many came to the church services in response to the reported healings. He would sometimes state in his altar calls, "Many of you came to have your sick bodies healed, but what about your sin-sick soul?" Skinner's propensity for winning souls and healing the sick converged together into one cohesive core.

Typically, there were at least fifty to seventy-five persons responding to the altar call in every service. There would be someone singing the "Invitation Song" as Skinner sometimes warned and other times pleaded with the unconverted to come and get saved before it is too late.

Those that came forward for salvation would stand at the altar and one of the ministers would have the potential converts repeat the "Sinners' Prayer." After which another minister prayed "the Prayer of Consecration" over the new converts.

Many Pentecostals celebrated Skinner's spiritual gifts. One of the gifts that were eminent in his ministry was the "Word of Knowledge." In Pentecostal and charismatic circles the Word of Knowledge is interpreted as the gift whereby the individual with this gift would know, *supernaturally*, what was going on in the person's life to whom he/she was ministering. The purpose was to build the faith of the person receiving prayer. The reasoning was that if God revealed his or her particular need to the minister then it made sense that God was going to meet that need, or why else would He reveal it?

Most of the time Skinner would administer this gift by choosing some of the new converts for special prayer; he would typically start by asking, "I don't know you do I?" The person usually responded either by shaking the head no or by replying, "No, you don't." At that point Skinner would describe something that was going on in their life, such as a condition they had or a current illness that was not obvious to the eyes. If it was too personal, he would whisper it in the ear. Then he would say, "I could not have known these things if God had not told me." The person would sometimes look amazed that he knew those things about them and at other times they wept.

There were other times when he moved among the audience and chose some for special prayer. Skinner would reveal some situation in their lives or "call out a condition." Skinner had remarked that he could sometimes feel the condition of the person, which is how he knew what the person was feeling. After praying for the infirmed individual, the condition would leave the person and him.

I recall one time we were walking through Kennedy International Airport about to take a trip overseas. As Skinner walked behind me I could hear him stop a stranger and ask, "I don't know you do I?" he then revealed some things about the woman and prayed for her right there in the airport.

On another occasion, I visited him in his office with two friends of mine. Upon entering his office, before my friend said a word, Skinner started revealing some things about my friend that not even I was aware of. My friend, startled by the things Skinner said to him, was uncharacteristically quiet after we left Skinner's office to have lunch. That night during the church service, Skinner asked him to stand and said to him, "I shocked you this afternoon when I told you those things about yourself, didn't I?" Skinner then prayed for him and requested that he return to see him again because he had additional things to tell him that the Lord had revealed. Unfortunately, he procrastinated going to see Skinner. To this day, he still regrets not going back to see what else Skinner had to say to him.

Many times, he warned persons of impending danger if they continued in their ways, and at other times, he gave an answer to an *unspoken* prayer request the person had before the Lord. Arturo also ministered in the prophetic. One pastor I knew from California told me that Skinner had come to California some years earlier and gave him a prophecy concerning the success of his church. According to this pastor, his membership suddenly "exploded" just as Skinner had predicted.

An example of a "prophetic word of warning" is the time a person I knew attended one of the crusades. Skinner chose him for special prayer from among those that came forward for salvation. It seems he had been involved with stealing cars. As Skinner addressed him, his eyes looked away as though he was visualizing something, and in a demonstrative style, Skinner began revealing the "vision." "I see you and some other guys opening the hood of a car...and now you are putting wires together." Skinner, acting as though he were putting wires together, went on to say, "Oh I see now, you all are stealing the car. I see the police chasing you all in their police car; they are pulling out their guns...they shoot!" and in dramatic fashion, he turned and pointed his finger at him and exclaimed, "And you got killed."

I later spoke with my acquaintance concerning his encounter

with Skinner and he told me that Skinner's prediction left him dumbfounded and petrified. So much so that he warned his partners in crime of the prophecy by Skinner and, according to him, they all "swore-off" their stealing of cars.

"Everyone Get Under the Blood"

As mentioned earlier, Skinner's ministry focused on the exor-cising of demons. When Skinner "discerned" that the person he was about to pray for was demon possessed, he would instruct the audience stating, "Everyone get under the blood [of Jesus]." This signaled the audience that a demon was about to be expelled from the individual receiving ministry. It was believed that if a demon was expelled and those in the audience were not "under the blood," they would become susceptible to demonic attack from the expelled demon. This belief was based on Luke, chapter eleven, where Jesus stated that when a demon is cast out, it goes in dry places looking for another home, i.e. another person to inhabit.

Sometime Skinner would call the "name" of the demon being expelled, e.g. a "snake spirit." Some of those being ministered to often made strange noises as Skinner commanded the demons to leave.

One of the incidents that remains indelibly etched in my mind is the time when Skinner was conducting a crusade in Trinidad, West Indies. There was a woman in the service that approached the stage while Skinner was praying for the people and began speaking to Skinner. She started at first speaking in a normal tone. I remember her saying, "Rev. Skinner" and then without warning went into a growl, and then continued again to speak in a normal tone as though nothing had happened. Skinner called her onto the stage. I was standing next to Skinner, directing the people as he was laying hands on them. Skinner began addressing the *demon*, commanding the demon to come out of her. With that, the lady screamed and fell out on the stage. As she laid there screaming, Skinner said some-thing to the effect that the demons were irritated and that was why *they* were screaming; they were on their way out.

A while later, the woman got up from the floor with a totally different demeanor. She was calm and thanked Skinner for his prayers. What comes to mind when I think of that incident is when Jesus cast out of a man a *legion* of demons. When the demons left, the Bible says that the man was "Clothed and in his right mind."

Healing Testimonies

As with most healing evangelists, when the healing portion of the service commenced, they would "ready" their audience for healing and Skinner did the same. Many times, he would ask those in the audience that God had healed under his ministry to come forward and give a testimony. The congregation understood that this was not the time for testimonies about how God healed under someone else's ministry. When those came forward to testify, he would typically ask, "What happened when I laid *my* hands on you?"

The person would give his or her testimony of a healing or an answer to prayer. I have heard him say that by doing this, he was attempting to stir-up the faith of those in the audience that were seeking to be healed. Arturo believed in laying his hands on the person, usually on their head, as he prayed. In many of the church services, he would lay hands on all those in attendance.

The following are some of the testimonies of healing that have occurred in the ministry of Arturo Skinner:

Norma was in a sanatorium suffering from tuberculosis. She was signed out of the hospital to attend a service conducted by Skinner. After Skinner prayed for her she returned to the sanatorium. After examining her, the doctors wanted to know what had happened to her; saying, "Whatever you did, her lungs are clearing up."

In another incident, there was a boy who suffered from spinal meningitis. Skinner picked the boy up in his arms and prayed for him and he was instantly healed from this disease that threatened his life.

As validation of Skinner's healing ministry, most often cited is the healing and deliverance of Penny Hooks. It is also an example of demonic activity in a person's life.

Clarence Taylor, reflecting on Skinner's healing and deliverance ministry, gives this account in his work, *The Black Churches of*

Brooklyn on the healing and deliverance of Penny Hooks:

As a young woman living in Harlem in 1962, Hooks was stricken with multiple sclerosis, which left her unable to walk. Her family took Hooks to several doctors, and she was eventually admitted to hospitals for treatment. However, Hooks' condition grew worse. She had screaming fits and threatened family members with bodily harm. After a brief stay at home, Hooks became deranged and violent and was finally admitted to the Psychiatric Ward at Harlem Hospital.

One Sunday, Hooks' mother met an old friend who told her about Arturo Skinner and how God worked through him to heal people. Mildred Hooks traveled to Brooklyn and spoke to Reverend Skinner, who assured her that everything would be all right and then went to the hospital to meet Penny Hooks. On February 21, 1963, Hooks was released from Harlem Hospital, and the Hooks family began attending [Saturday] services at Deliverance Evangelistic Center in Brooklyn. Eventually, Hooks' family began accepting the notion that her suffering was due to spiritual, not medical reason. According to her sister, Esther Hooks, Penny was demon possessed. Skinner used prayer and anointed her with oil. Gradually, Hooks began to improve. By October 1963, her mental faculties were restored. She regained her speech and the violent outbursts stopped. By the fall of 1964, Hooks began to walk.

Before Penny was healed, some people in the church complained about Penny's violent outbursts during the service. Skinner ignored the complaints. As far as Skinner was concerned, God said that Penny was going to one day march in the choir and he was not going to back-off what he claimed God had showed him.

Although there were scores healed of all sorts of infirmities, not everyone prayed for by Skinner received healing. I will not speculate here on why everyone he, or anyone else, had prayed for were not healed. It is impossible to respond with certainty, as there are too many variables to consider. I will respond, however, to those who have unjustly criticized Skinner by inferring that if his gift was so great, why some of his close associates died or why his blind half-brother had not been healed.

I invite the reader to consider this, when God heals someone, we should give God the glory. However, many times when God does *not* heal, we hold responsible and sometimes ridicule the individual that prayed for the infirmed person. It is only reasonable that if one should not assume the credit for the healing, then neither should he/she be held accountable when healing does not occur. No matter how great one's "gift" is, he/she is not the one that determines who God heals and who He does not heal.

Central Av Center

President .... SIS. ESTELLE RAY
Vice President .... BRO. WARREN
Secretary .... SIS. HENRIETTA WILLIAMS
Financial Secretary .... SIS. JEAN SIMMONS
Treasurer .... SIS. BEATRICE GOODMAN
Chaplain .... MOTHER ALICE WILLIAMS
This Choir is under the directorship of SIS. MIRIAM JACKSON.

DEC Choir 1959

DEC Choir 1965

DBI 1959

Deliverance Temple

CHAPTER THREE

Man of God, Son of Thunder

Not that ...I have already been made perfect...Brothers, I do
not consider myself yet to have taken hold of it. But one thing
I do: ...I press on toward the goal to win the prize for which
God has called me heavenward in Christ Jesus.

Apostle Paul, Philippians 3:12-14

When Skinner felt deprived of his rights, he would sometimes go into a burst of rage demanding satisfaction. My first experience witnessing one of his outbursts was after a church service on a Saturday night, when he had given one of the children money to buy ice-cream. When the store clerk refused to give the youngster what he wanted (he wanted his ice-cream mixed with two different flavors), the child informed Skinner. Being informed that the clerk would not give the child what he wanted, Skinner went to the store, which was located in proximity to the church, and in a rage shouted at the storeowner informing him that the church puts thousands of dollars into his establishment. In addition, Skinner threatened the storeowner stating that if he did not give the child what he wanted that the church would boycott the restaurant. By this time, a crowd from the church had gathered, observing what was happening and egging Skinner on; the boy got his ice cream.

Skinner appeared to be fearless. At times, however, he was careless with his courage. In one incident after a church service, one of the young men from the neighborhood pulled a gun on one of the members of the church. As Skinner was leaving to go home, one of the church members ran to his car and made him aware of the situation. By all accounts, Skinner jumped out of his car, ran over to the young man with the gun and with one blow with his fist knocked him down. Not long after the incident, this same young man was assisting Skinner in the pulpit. Skinner proudly boasted, "I bopped this boy right [to] my side."

Skinner also possessed a competitive nature. According to one insider, Skinner enjoyed the distinction of being first to accomplish some achievement. Although Skinner did not have much of a formal education, he was an astute businessman and a master negotiator. On one occasion, one of the pastors was buying a building for his church sanctuary. Skinner was there at the negotiations and took charge mandating the terms to the owner. Skinner often would lend money to pastors that were buying property for their churches, at no interest. One of the ministers I interviewed stated that he witnessed Skinner conduct an entire business transaction in Hebrew [sic].

The Consummate Promoter

Image to Skinner was very important; he raised the quality of advertising for much of the black churches in general. Many things taken for granted today began with Skinner. For example, in the past churches advertised using a low-grade tissue-like quality paper called a "throw away." According to Charles Gill, a professional photographer who serviced numerous churches for many years, and others I have spoken to, claim that Skinner was the first to begin using the shiny stock paper and clear high-quality photos for his advertisements. Skinner used to say, "I wouldn't put out an advertisement that I wouldn't want to receive."

Capitalizing on his experience in show business and advertising skills, the churches sponsoring special events, as when the renowned African evangelist Nicholas Benghu held a meeting in the United States, typically called upon Skinner to handle the advertising.

As a brilliant advertiser, Skinner would often profit from current trends by modifying his advertising. For instance, when the motion picture "The Exorcist" became popular in the early 1970s Skinner was already exorcising demons. He merely adjusted his advertising to capitalize on the publicity of the film by advertising his Saturday night services as "Exorcism Services." According to one insider, Skinner also liberally borrowed ideas from other magazines, both secular and religious.

Another example of him capitalizing on the latest trend was the title that he adopted in the early 1970s. At first, he deemed himself as "God's Apostle and Your Servant," but later "redefined" himself as "God's Modern Day Black Apostle." In the magazine that first introduced his new title, he was quick to quell any misunderstanding by stating a disclaimer, which said in effect, that he was not an apostle just for black people, but a black apostle for all people.

He was not only a creative advertiser, but also a consummate promoter. He used his skills of persuasion to convince people that they should attend the service. Even after the meeting was over, he was still promoting the service by making one believe they had missed a great move of God by not attending the service. The strategy behind his "post promotion" was to build an air of expectancy for the next deliverance church service.

One of the former employees of the Public Relations Department of the church informed me that Skinner said to him that if he only had enough money to do one thing, he would spend it on advertising. I imagine if Skinner had not been a preacher he could have been successful as a promoter.

As a promoter Skinner knew that he needed to keep the image of the church in the minds of the public. One of the ways of doing that was with the printed page. The church had a magazine called the "Deliverance Messenger," later changed to the "Deliverance Voice." In it, one would find a message from Skinner along with testimonies of healing and Skinner's itinerary among other things. The circulation for the magazine at his death was one hundred and fifty thousand readers.

Along with the church's magazine were banners and buttons with the scripture that read, "No weapon formed against you shall prosper." Included on the banner would also be the name of the church.

Most Christian churches have the American flag alongside the

Christian flag. In Deliverance, there was an additional flag with a large red cross across the front of a sky-blue background. Evangelist Hazel Scott, who was its designer, presented the "Deliverance Flag" to Skinner on March 10, 1966.

All of the printing and the mailing was done in-house. In-house printing served three purposes: Skinner could have total control of what was going on and not be at the mercy of an outside firm and their errors of multiple mailings to the same person, he could keep his mailing list secure and he could train and employ more of the youths and adults of the church. Many of those trained at the Deliverance offices have gone on and obtained secular employment using the skills they received at the church office.

Crosses in the Windows

In December of 1972, crosses began mysteriously appearing in the church windows at the Deliverance Temple in Newark that Skinner claimed were angels, which was consistent with his belief in the God of the supernatural. Skinner believed God could and *would* give supernatural signs as in the Bible. Even though some thought that the crosses in the windows were more of a natural occurrence than a supernatural phenomenon it did not prevent Skinner from capitalizing on the incident. Being the adept advertiser that he was, when people came from all over the City of Newark and nearby areas to see the crosses in the windows, the members of the church were given the opportunity to pass out religious tracts and advertisements to them. Somehow, a rumor spread stating that Skinner was charging money for people to come and see the crosses so that he could line his pockets with the proceeds. One of the local radio personalities, Roy West of WPAT, in an interview with Rev. Jesse Jackson, repeated the hearsay as fact on his (West's) radio broadcast.

During this time, coincidentally, Skinner was looking to purchase a radio station. Skinner made the church aware of the bogus charges by West and remarking in jest stated, "You all know I am looking for a radio station to purchase; God works in mysterious ways." Implying, this may be the way he will obtain a radio station by suing WPAT for slander.

Skinner invited West to the church and West recanted his statements on radio and apologized to Skinner and the Deliverance church, bestowing praise for the work Skinner was doing in the community. The following is part of his statement, as recorded in Lockwood's book:

"Two weeks ago, I made an unfair criticism of Reverend Arturo Skinner when I talked about the crosses that mysteriously appeared in the windows of his church on Clinton Avenue in December of 1972...it is not true that Reverend Skinner charged people to see the crosses... The source of the crosses are of little importance when measured against the works of Reverend Skinner and the church...." (Lockwood 1976)

A Letter to My Enemies

It would be naive to suppose with all that Skinner possessed, that his success would not foster resentments among some ministers and laypersons alike. While no one is above criticism, several people who criticized Skinner were motivated by jealously and ill-will. In an attempt to mar his reputation and diminish his influence, they would spread untruths and malicious rumors. Others, although sincere, misread his intentions and made misinformed character judgments. On the other hand, some of the criticisms were not without merit.

For example, Skinner often railed against his enemies to the point of appearing paranoid at times. In addition, Skinner had difficulty at times being objective, especially when it came to those with whom he trusted. There were times when those he trusted would bring false allegations to him about others and he would accept as true the accusations without further investigation. This led to Skinner falsely accusing people of actions to which there was no basis in fact and wrongly condemning them as his enemies.

There were also the "momentary enemies," those in which he was angry with for the *moment*, just as a mother or father would get irritated and may tell their son or daughter to get out of their sight. Skinner sometimes employed the expression "enemy" to convey his disapproval for something someone may or may not have done.

As one member I interviewed stated, "There were times when it appeared as though he was impossible to please, no matter how well one performed [his or her] task." To make matters worse, Skinner was vociferous when he reprimanded others. Those who were acquainted with him knew that he was just "blowing off steam" and that his anger would be short-lived, nonetheless knowing that did not ease the sting of his reproof.

Be that as it may, Skinner wrote an open letter to his enemies, both real and contrived thanking them for the lies they spread on him and their opposition to his ministry. He noted that if it were not for their opposition his ministry would not have been as successful.

Skinner and Theological Debates

As a practice Skinner did not engage in theological deliberations. However, on at least one occasion he decided to field some questions from the audience in relation to the deliverance ministry. During this session, an individual from the audience asked him if a demon can possess a Christian and Skinner responded "Yes." The person then repeated the question as though he did not hear the reply Skinner gave the first time, again, he answered, "Yes" to the astonishment of myself, the teachers of D.B.I, and, I am sure, others in the audience. One of the reasons for the incredulity at his response is that Skinner had not taught, prior to this time, the demonization of Christians nor had he mentioned exorcising demons out of Christians. Besides that, D.B.I, of which Skinner was the president, held the position that a demon *cannot* inhabit a Christian.

The following Tuesday in Bible school the teachers were scrambling for an explanation. I inquired of one of the D.B.I. teachers concerning Skinner's statement. The explanation I received was that, "What [Rev Skinner] *really* meant was that a Christian can be *oppressed* by the devil, but not *possessed*." One of the Bible school-teachers informed me that when she attempted to get clarification from Skinner concerning his response to the question, he would only say, "I said what I said now you look it up." As far as Skinner was concerned, the issue was closed. All the same, even though Skinner did not offer a retraction to his statement, the D.B.I position on the matter remained unchanged. According to my information, Skinner never raised the issue again.

It is safe to assume that Skinner reconsidered his position in regard to demons inhabiting Christians based on the fact that he did not bring the subject up again in addition to D.B.I continuing to teach that demons cannot inhabit Christians.

Skinner never married although one might imagine many women joined Deliverance with intentions of becoming Mrs. Skinner one day. I remember one deluded woman claimed that she was Mrs. Skinner and demanded that she sit in the pulpit next to him.

In an interview with Myrna Hallenbeck, a member of Deliverance from its inception, she stated that she asked Skinner why he was not married. According to Hallenbeck, he informed her that he would never get married. Quoting Skinner she said, "The work that God is calling me to, no woman will be able to understand my drive." One female evangelist, who had romantic intentions toward Skinner stated, "Those [church] people are going to cause him to miss his blessing."

Conflict at PDC

Skinner's strong personality many times put him on a collision course with other people who exhibited a similar strength in their character, and at times it has led to the inevitable impact.

One such incident occurred in 1969 in which a major rift occurred between Arturo Skinner and Harold Benjamin, the pastor of the Pennsylvania Deliverance Center (P.D.C.). This conflict resulted in Skinner resolving to remove Benjamin as pastor. However, Benjamin was not willing to step down from his pastorate without resistance. As a result, a public clash ensued with each accusing the other of wrongdoing.

There are conflicting accounts as to the cause for the dispute. Skinner claimed there was a conspiracy taking place. According to Skinner, the alleged conspiracy included Benjamin and two close associates, John Meyers and Richard White, two ministers in Deliverance. In addition, Richard Henton of Chicago, a long-time friend of Skinner, engaged Benjamin and White as guest preachers at his church. In Skinner's eyes this implicated Henton as a co-conspirator. Skinner often stated, "You can't be my friend hanging out with my enemies."

Even though prior to the dispute, it was Skinner that brought Benjamin and White to Henton's attention, Skinner felt that since he and Henton were long-time friends, along with being Henton's pastor, that Henton should have trusted him and canceled any future preaching engagements of Benjamin and White.

Consequently, a number of the laity and ministers felt compelled to choose sides. Although many had been friends for years, they thought it not wise to publically affiliate with one another.

The Benjamin supporters accused Skinner of being unreasonable and the alleged conspiracy an invention of his own paranoia. According to one insider, the true reason he implicated Henton as a co-conspirator was his (Henton) association with John Wilson, a pastor from Connecticut who refused Skinner's offer to join the Deliverance fellowship.

After much controversy, Benjamin was removed from his pastorate. However, Benjamin was still popular among the ministers in Philadelphia and the members at P.D.C. Consequently, with Benjamin's removal, along with the stigma of a public church upheaval, the attendance fell off dramatically from close to four-hundred to less than twenty persons on Sunday morning.

Subsequent to Skinner removing Benjamin as pastor, Skinner sent evangelists from his church down to Philadelphia to conduct services during the week. Skinner would personally conduct services at P.D.C. every Sunday morning at eleven a.m. with many of those that left during the controversy returning. While it never did achieve its former glory, according to a former member of P.D.C., the attendance on Sunday mornings grew close to three-hundred. Rev. John Blaine, who was one of those ministering at P.D.C. after Benjamin was deposed, states that the congregation began to increase. However, after Skinner's death, the attendance again fell off.

In succeeding years, there were efforts to revive P.D.C. However all of the labor amounted to nothing more than an exercise in futility, and eventually those few that remained in the congregation disbanded, leaving the building abandoned.

Some of those I spoke with during the time of the dispute were hoping and praying for reconciliation between Skinner and Henton. Sadly the reconciliation never materialized. Skinner died never having made peace with his long-time friend.

In two separate interviews with Matthew Johnson, Skinner's former driver, and Richard Henton, both claimed that Skinner had been "done wrong repeatedly by others." Based on their revelation, I surmise that Skinner had become distrustful of others because of past betrayals of some of those whom he trusted.

"Touch Not Mine Anointed..."

Many black Pentecostal churches pride themselves on being a theocracy, i.e., God, not a trustee board or board of directors governs them. The stories of trustees ruining the church by opposing the vision of the pastor were common among those "other" churches. It was believed in many Pentecostal churches that the Lord would lead the pastor, especially if he/she was the founder, and the members would follow suit. Although there were people assigned as trustees, in many cases they followed the wishes of the pastor.

Case in point, in one prominent Pentecostal church, in a Bible class in which I was present, the pastor related a past dispute he had with his board of trustees. This pastor stated that the Lord was leading him to build a new church edifice and the trustee board opposed the idea and would not release the monies. The pastor said he simply fired the entire board and chose a board that would acquiesce to his wishes.

In Deliverance, there was no question that Arturo Skinner was the one in charge. On the other hand, in Skinner's defense, it was hard to argue with his success. Under his watch, the church was prospering and growing, plus all the bills were paid on time.

Skinner would never have had the temerity to claim infallibility. However, the congregation considered him a man anointed by God. In the Bible there is a verse found in First Chronicles 16:22, which reads, "Touch not mine anointed and do my prophets no harm." The interpretation by most Pentecostals indicates that if anyone was to "touch" God's anointed by means of opposing him/her by word or deed, that (s)he would incur God's wrath and punishment. Skinner reinforced this notion repeatedly, via accounts of those who opposed him and the fate they supposedly received for their rebelliousness.

Furthermore, many in the church had a problem separating Apostle Skinner, the *man of God* from Arturo Skinner *the man.* If Skinner said it, as far as they were concerned, he got it from God.

In contrast, what many did not realize was that Skinner had a great sense of humor that he would display to some of the members. One young man in the church told me of an incident with Skinner. On this occasion Skinner stormed out of his office yelling at him at the top of his voice for no apparent reason. The young man startled by this sudden occurrence of anger asked Skinner, "What did I do?" Skinner laughed and replied, "Nothing, I just haven't yelled at anyone today."

Skinner also had a great compassion for the poor, not just in his neighborhood, but throughout the nation as well. When Skinner visited a new town, he would ask those that were showing him around to take him to the poorest part of town. After viewing the area, he would report back to the missionaries in the church and instruct them to start a mission outreach there. The Deliverance church had mission outreaches across the country, and started or supported many other missions in foreign countries as well.

Skinner's personality would not allow for indifference. If one knew Skinner, whatever one's feelings toward him were, those feelings did not include apathy. Skinner's eccentricities would often take us on an emotional rollercoaster, through a series of highs and lows. We would often question his actions, and at the same time extol his love; disdain his stubbornness but applaud his persistence; loathe what we considered to be his arrogance, but embrace the self-esteem he inspired in us; condemn his anger, but commend his compassion. As one pastor stated, speaking of Skinner after his death, and I suppose he said it best, "I am going to miss him... he was not a perfect man, but he was a good man."

DELIVERANCE FLAG UNVEILED

March 10th 1966: Evang. Hazel Scott, the flag's designer, presented the Deliverance flag to Pastor Skinner

Dr. Edward Hallenbeck

CHAPTER FOUR

The Greatest Supernatural Happening...

> *The people that do know their God shall be strong and carry out great exploits.*
>
> (Daniel 11:32b NKJV)

There were people whose talents and personalities stood out from among the many other talented persons. These persons usually had a profoundly memorable effect on those that attended Deliverance. In doing research for this book, by means of reminiscing with others about their experiences in Deliverance, these persons I am about to refer to were most commonly among those mentioned.

One of those of note that joined Deliverance from another ministry was Martha Doretha Everett. She joined in 1959 and played an important role in the success of the church. Everett was invited by Professor Francis Madison, a concert pianist, to do a special solo for the choir. As a transfer from the First Church of God in Christ located in Brooklyn, with her mellow soprano tonality she was celebrated as the "Golden voice of Deliverance."

In 1958, Skinner organized the Deliverance Bible Institute (D.B.I). Arturo, recognizing his formal educational limitations, generally deferred questions of a theological nature to Dr. Edward Hallenbeck—the dean of D.B.I. Hallenbeck's talents and scriptural knowledge was the perfect complement to Skinner's charisma.

Skinner would attract new converts while Hallenbeck and the D.B.I. faculty instructed them in the Bible.

A former pastor of the United Holiness Church, Hallenbeck excelled at making complex biblical concepts understandable. Strangely enough, Hallenbeck died on March 20, 1974, the same day one year prior to Skinner's death.

Common in Pentecostal churches is the testimony portion of the service in which the audience participates by testifying and spontaneously singing "congregational" choruses. Song leaders direct the testimony portion of the service as they keep the services lively. Two of those whose talents stood out among the other talented song leaders in Deliverance were Joseph (Jo-Jo) Tab, a former Brooklyn gang member and Richard (Richie) White, whose signature bald-head and brawn earned him the nick-name "Mr. Clean."

In addition to them, there was William (Billy) Wooten, the choir director who stood a commanding six foot six inches tall. His flair and theatrics in directing the nearly five-hundred voice choir was renowned in many church circles. Some visiting the church came in response to the reputation of this extraordinary choir director.

The "Deliverance Stars"

The soloists and singing groups, and there were many, were coined by Skinner as the "Deliverance Stars." They sang in most of the services and performed individual concerts. Traces of his show business background were evident as he assigned a manager who was in charge of setting up the concerts for the Deliverance Stars. The manager for the Deliverance Stars, Jasper Samuel, was a young man who grew up in the Marcy Projects in Brooklyn. He was chosen from among those in the congregation and trained by Skinner. Skinner made it a point of training individuals from within the church and, if necessary, sending those in consideration for the positions to school.

Deliverance owned its own record label where many of the Deliverance Stars made their recordings. The church purchased the rights to a few of the Deliverance Stars' original compositions. Perhaps Skinner was attempting to live out his past show business ambitions vicariously through the Deliverance Stars. Besides, the soloists and singing groups, there was the one-hundred voice all male chorus.

In addition, there was a fifteen-piece band and forty-five-piece orchestra, headed by the mother and son team of Jacqueline and Kenneth Hicks. These were made-up of members of the church, both adults and young people.

Women in Deliverance

As with most churches, women play an important role in the development, and many times, the success of the church. This statement is no less accurate as it pertains to the Deliverance church. Without the contributions of several women, the ministry would not have enjoyed the success that it did.

One of those women was Emmaline Moe, a woman of means who contributed greatly financially to the Deliverance church. The "Volunteers of Deliverance," who supported the ministry financially, was the brainchild of Moe.

Doris Miller-Lundy, a prominent figure in Deliverance, was gifted with great administration skills and she used her talents unselfishly to advance the Deliverance church. For a time, she was the directress of the Deliverance Conventions, executive director of the "Hour of Deliverance" radio program, faculty member of D.B.I, and confidante to Skinner. In addition to them were Corrine Austin, Louise Durant, Maude Heywood, Ethel Askew, Carrie Black and Carrie Simmons, among many others.

With some exceptions, black Pentecostal organizations, while allowing women to teach in their churches, would not ordain women. One notable exception to this ban, at least in C.O.G.I.C., was if the pastor was the husband, and if he was to expire, his wife could temporarily assume the role of pastor. In response to this prohibition of the ordination of women, some women preachers established their own churches and ministries independent of any major Pentecostal organization.

Skinner, in contrast, not only ordained women as pastors and ministers, but also encouraged women to become ministers. In the

Deliverance fellowship there were several woman pastors such as Elizabeth Ray in Jamaica, New York, Eleanor Pratt in Philadelphia, Pennsylvania, and Mary Parker Barnes of Rocky Mount, North Carolina, just to name a few. There were also full-time women evangelists. Some of the younger female preachers, whose ages ranged from sixteen to twenty-five years of age, largely preached at various churches in the vicinity. The only public distinction Skinner made in opposition to women in ministry was the office of apostle. Skinner did not ordain, nor did he advocate women becoming apostles.

Along with the pioneering women were some pioneering men such as George Cherry, crusade manager for the "Christ is the Answer" crusades, trustee member, church sexton, and along with Matthew Johnson and Fred Little, radio technician for the Hour of Deliverance broadcast.

Another important figure in Deliverance was Skinner's cousin, Kenneth Griffith, the Director of the Executive Offices and president of the Deliverance Businessmen's Fellowship. These are just four of the many men that contributed greatly to the success of the Deliverance Evangelistic Center church.

Skinner and Education

Skinner encouraged his young people to get an education. In an interview with Dr. Lucille Oliver-Bellow, she had made up her mind that she was going to join the Air Force. Skinner told her that God said that she was to go to college and become a teacher. When the Air Force recruiter called her home, the people she lived with informed the recruiter that she was not going to join. When she returned home and they informed her of what happened they told her Skinner instructed them to do it.

She asked Skinner why he instructed them to cancel her appointment at the recruiter's office. Skinner informed her that God said she was to go to college. She applied to college and got a rejection letter. Disappointed after her rejection, she went back to Skinner and complained. Skinner did not give her any encouragement. As far as he was concerned, God said she was to be a teacher and the issue was closed.

Later that week, to her amazement, she received an acceptance letter from the college that rejected her earlier. However, she wanted to study medicine, but Skinner told her God wanted her to teach. She took some pre-med courses, despite what Skinner said, and failed, but did well in her English courses. Today she has an Ed. D. (Doctor of Education) degree and credits Skinner's guidance for her accomplishments. While this was not typical, it does demonstrate the importance he placed upon education.

Skinner did not share the same enthusiasm for higher education for his ministers however. Influenced by the Pentecostal point of view, he was concerned that those that attended seminary would compromise, and in many instances lose their faith. Bible seminaries many times were derided as "Bible cemeteries." I remember the accounts of those that attended seminary and after attending no longer believed in the inerrancy of the Bible.

However, Skinner did open doors for the novice preacher. To some of the graduates of Zion Bible Institute, along with others, he gave opportunities to perfect their craft at the Deliverance Center.

Skinner also trained many of the young inspiring preachers by allowing them to be a part of his personal mentoring class called the "School of the Prophets" and to become a "Junior Pastor." The Junior Pastors were there to assist Skinner in the pulpit and on occasion traveled with him on the many crusades that he conducted.

How much more readily we imitate those whom we like can scarcely be expressed.

—Quintilian

Arturo had a distinctive way of speaking which was often mimicked by those (especially the young men) in the church; some out of admiration and others for amusement. Ironically, those who made it a part of their usual way of speaking or adopted his gestures when they preached were criticized for "trying to be like the apostle."

The mimicking was not limited to the way he spoke. Many ministers and lay-members that admired him copied his walk and stately mannerisms. Many of the young men in the church dressed attempting to mimic Skinner's stylishness.

out to dinner with some of those who were "raised" by
ould often say to one that acted contrary, "You know
˻˻˻˻ ˻ᴋ˻˻ner taught us better than that." He taught us how to act
with dignitaries, how to dress for special occasions, even what to tip
the waiters in a restaurant.

Charismatic Renewal

"Pentecostalism is the only denomination of the Christian faith
in the United States founded by African American people." Ithiel
Clemmons, *Bishop C.H. Mason and the Roots of the Church of God
in Christ*

Most African American Pentecostal churches worship in the tradition of the "slave religion." *The Dictionary of Pentecostal and
Charismatic Movement* explains:

"It should be stated on the onset that it is primarily in worship
form, religious expression, and lifestyle rather than a codified belief
system that the Black Holiness Pentecostalism shares in the rich tradition and legacy of black slave religion."

In the early 1960s it appeared as though the healing revival,
which in its genesis mostly attracted the poorly educated and the
underprivileged, was ending. Many of the post WWII healing revivalists had folded their tents and disappeared off the scene. Around
the late 1960s to early 1970s, the mainline churches and the more
sophisticated people started accepting speaking in tongues and other
spiritual gifts along with casting out demons, though not abandoning
their reserved demeanor. These people were coined neo-Pentecos-
tals (a.k.a. charismatic). "The neo-Pentecostal preachers were more
erudite their message was more complicated and less given to novel
and simplistic biblical exegesis...." (Harrell 1978)

In the early 1970s, I attended a large charismatic meeting in
Pittsburg, Pennsylvania, and was introduced to the term "soulish
worship," used pejoratively and defined as emotional (i.e. non-spir-
itual) worship. I could not help feeling they were impugning the
African American "slave religion" manner of worship.

Skinner did not "sophisticate" his meetings to accommodate the
charismatic movement, but continued in the slave religion tradition

of the black Pentecostal church. However, in 1974 he did change the name of the Bible School from the "Deliverance Bible Institute" to the "Charismatic Soul-Winners Bible Institute." With the change in name, there also came a change in the way the Bible School functioned. The classes were no longer split-up into different subjects, but became one class. In addition, the Bible School began focusing more on the Holy Spirit and spiritual gifts.

Skinner did not publically criticize the charismatic movement, but did express disappointment when the Pentecostal and healing evangelist giant, Oral Roberts, left the Pentecostal church and joined the Boston Avenue Methodist church in 1968.

Skinner continued drawing large crowds to his services despite the end of the healing revival and popularity of the "Charismatic Renewal." Annually, Skinner conducted his "Christ is the Answer" crusades at the Rockland Palace auditorium located on 155th Street in Harlem, NY. With the demolishing of Rockland Palace, Skinner took his ministry to the next level in 1971, by moving his crusade from Harlem to bustling midtown Manhattan. The Felt Forum auditorium at Madison Square Garden was the new venue for the crusade. This was a strategic move affording his ministry greater visibility. The Felt Forum had a seating capacity of five-thousand. Positioned adjacent to New York's Pennsylvania Station, it was easily accessible with many trains of the New York City and New Jersey transit converging there. However, this was not his first crusade in midtown. On Saturday, October 16, 1965, Skinner had a crusade at the Manhattan Center, located across the street from Felt Forum.

In an interview with one of those that counted the offering at the first Felt Forum crusade, she said Skinner came to where they were counting and said, "Look what God has done for us. We must be careful to stay humble."

Skinner also held a series of meetings on Monday nights at the Audubon Ballroom in Harlem where the Black Nationalist, Malcolm X had been assassinated a few years prior. I recall the catchy slogan he had for the Audubon meetings; "Everybody knows, where everybody goes on Monday night," then he cued the audience, "Where children?" and the audience responded in unison, "The Audubon."

Skinner typically had a different theme for each crusade, e.g.,

"Christ is the Answer," "A Supernatural Christ for a Superficial World," and "Back to God," among others. As the reports of healing began to increase, so did the crowds.

"The Greatest Supernatural Happening that will Change Your Entire Life"

In 1972, Skinner took a bold step of faith. Here was a man who only a mere twenty years prior was a drug abuser, a virtual unknown to the church world and contemplating suicide. Now he was attempting something never before achieved by a black Pentecostal preacher—a four-night crusade (July 6-9) in the main arena of the world-renowned Madison Square Garden (M.S.G.), coined "The Greatest Supernatural Happening that will Change Your Entire Life."

I remember when he first announced that the church was going to the main arena. Admittedly, I thought that he had really over-played his hand. First, no Pentecostal preacher, let alone a black Pentecostal preacher, had ever attempted this. Madison Square Garden seats twenty thousand people just in the stands alone not counting the playing floor, which could probably seat another two-thousand. Up until that time, the most crowds he attracted in his crusades were five-thousand. Even if ten-thousand persons attended the event, it would be a mockery. Skinner needed mass media appeal and he had never advertised on this grand scale before.

Secondly, while "The Hour of Deliverance" radio broadcast went across the country and around the world, he was only on radio for a half hour, twice a week in the New York tri-State area. Christian television was in its infancy so there were no Christian television stations to promote the crusade.

Moreover, when it came near the time for the crusade, the foremost gospel DJ in New York at the time—Joe Bostic, Jr., did little to promote the meeting. Typically, Bostic made personal promos for up-coming events in the African American church community. However, when announcing the Madison Square Garden crusade, he would only say "Now this" and then play a pre-recorded tape that the church had made. The basis for this "snub" was that Bostic called the church and requested that Skinner include some of the popular gospel artists that were going to be in New York during the time of the crusade. Even though this was a major church event and a first of its kind in the African American community, when Skinner did not comply with his request, Bostic exercised his option not to personally promote the crusade.

To add to that, the Church of God in Christ, the largest African American Pentecostal church in the world, was in New York City not far from M.S.G. conducting their "Youth Congress" meeting during the same time of the crusade.

To make matters worse, some churches discouraged their people from supporting the crusade, and even some members of Deliverance opposed the idea of having such a large crusade and spoke against it.

Skinner knew that without the support of the churches and the support of others not familiar with his church or him, attendance for the meeting would be relatively poor. He needed to advertise this meeting on a mammoth scale. According to Jerome Boyde, who at the time worked in the Public Relations Department of the church, all of the artwork and layout for the crusade was handled in-house. Skinner had never marketed on this scale before, so Boyde suggested that the church use a bright orange color background for the church's posters to draw attention to them. These posters were on the buses of Manhattan and strategically placed in the subways throughout New York City. Also, the "Fore-runners," the church's street team, was out in full-force around M.S.G. promoting the crusade.

Prior to the crusade, Skinner held smaller meetings at auditoriums through-out the boroughs of New York City in promotion of the M.S.G. meeting. In addition to that people from all over the country that were familiar with Skinner planned their vacations around this history-making event.

As the time approached for the first night of the crusade, the anticipation grew. On the opening night close to eighteen-thousand people attended the crusade. For the next two nights the crowds increased and on the final day, held on Sunday afternoon, judging from the seating, more than twenty-thousand people attended. The altar filled nightly with literally multitudes of people coming from all over the arena to receive Christ. I suppose if he had the television coverage that many of the ministers have today, there would have been a turn-away crowd at the crusade.

Some of the many other places he held crusades were Yale University in New Haven, Connecticut, Cobo Hall in Detroit, Michigan, and the Oakland Arena in Oakland, California. Many other auditoriums, schools, and churches across the country hosted crusades as well with each attracting large crowds.

Before the M.S.G. crusade, Skinner was in negotiations to purchase Temple B'nai Abraham (T.B.A.) located at 621 Clinton Avenue. in Newark, New Jersey. It had a seating capacity of twenty-five-hundred, was equipped with a dining room, a smaller auditorium (seating four-hundred), an office building, a gym, and a pool.

According to one inside source, the purchase of T.B.A. did not come without opposition from the community. T.B.A. was being leased by the Newark Board of Education and was occupied with students. Consequently, if the church purchased the property the students would be displaced. When the news was made public that the church was purchasing the property, some people in the community whose children attended T.B.A. were up in arms.

A meeting was called for the community and the board to appeal to Skinner with the intent of convincing him not to purchase the property. Several people in the community and representatives of the board were allowed to speak and air their grievances. Arturo Skinner was always privileged to have those in his congregation that were familiar with certain business affairs. In this meeting, one of the members of the church, Elizabeth Irvin, who was involved in real estate for many years, stood in defense of the church.

T.B.A. was in disrepair and when Skinner took the stage to speak, he pointed out the poor condition of the building and reprimanded the board for housing students in a building that was in such a deplorable condition.

After Skinner made his case, some of those in the community were still opposed to him purchasing the property. In the face of the opposition from the community, the church purchased T.B.A. debt free.

With the overwhelming success of the M.S.G. crusade and the purchase of T.B.A, 1972 was a banner year for Deliverance.

Renamed the Deliverance Temple, it became the new headquarters.

According to the Deliverance web site, in 2006 the Deliverance Temple received landmark status by the New Jersey Historic Sites Review Board. In 2007 it was added to the National Trust for Historic Places with the designation of "National Significance."

James Blocker and Apostle Skinner at the Waldorf Astoria NYC. July 12, 1965

Kenneth Griffith

Martha Doretha Everett

CHAPTER FIVE

Arturo Skinner and the Black Power Movement

The most important contribution of the Black Power concept was the recognition of the political and economic control of the land.

—Gayraud S. Wilmore,
"Black Power and Black Radicalism"

During the decades of the 1960s and 1970s, the "Black Power Movement" came into prominence and promoted black pride. As a result, there arose an Afro-centric mind-set among many African Americans. Blacks were taking pride in the fact that they were of African descent with many exchanging their "slave names" (names inherited or given to their ancestors by the slave masters) for those that reflected their African heritage, and the wearing of African garb as a symbol of the unshackling from Western-colonialism.

The Black Power Movement also affected the black church. A popular book entitled, *Your God is Too White*, written by the bi-racial authorship of Columbus Salley and Ronald Behm, exposed some of the racism and hypocrisy of white "Christians," stating: "The Black man who wants to think independently cannot allow the white 'Christian' |sic| society, which has lied about and lied to blacks, to define the Christian faith for him." Also in 1967, a young evangelist, Bill Pannell, authored a controversial book entitled *My*

Friend the Enemy. One reviewer of this work stated, "For the first time, white evangelicals around the country were presented with the way black Christians really felt about their one-sided message..."

Several African American Pentecostals began questioning white ministers asking: "Why is there nothing in your gospel said about the poor or black people?" For many black Pentecostals, there was no relevance of the white minister's message to the black community.

Skinner possessed the unique ability of appealing to both the traditional and radical Pentecostal. By emphasizing prayer, holiness of life, and with the demonstration of spiritual gifts, he appealed to traditional Pentecostal ideals, while on the other hand appealing to the radical Pentecostal. Skinner advocated the mind-set of "Let's get our own stuff," which not only appealed to the radical Pentecostal but also attracted many of those not associated with the church. Alfred Sharpton, the civil rights activist, who at that time was a minister at the Washington Temple Church of God in Christ, frequently visited the Deliverance Center.

Racists Attitudes Among Pentecostals

In 1906, black and white Pentecostals worshiped together. Frank Bartleman, a white Pentecostal and witness to the Azusa St. revival, in referring to the revival stated, "The color line was washed away by the blood." Sadly, however, that was short-lived. The white Pentecostals caved in to the mores of the racially segregated South. Skinner had many white supporters of his ministry; even so, Skinner sometimes mentioned the disparities between the black and white races, which caused some to accuse him of not liking white people.

There are racial incidences that may have contributed to the views Skinner had in reference to racism in Pentecostal churches. For instance, according to the *Encyclopedia of African American Religions*:

"A group of Black congregations withdrew from the predominately White Assemblies of God (A.G.) in 1924 because of its refusal to sponsor African American missionaries to Africa. In 1924, they formed the United Pentecostal Council of the Assemblies of God (U.P.C.A.G.)...."

Bethel Gospel Tabernacle, Skinner's former church affiliation, was a member of the U.P.C.A.G. Along with Bob Harrison, a black minister in A.G. and an associate of Skinner, was denied ordination until Baptist evangelist Billy Graham invited him to join his evangelistic team in 1962. "Somewhat embarrassed, the A.G. moved quickly to ordain Harrison." The irony is Charles H. Mason, a black minister and founder of the C.O.G.I.C., ordained many of the early A.G. ministers.

However, the core of Skinner's message never strayed from a traditional salvation gospel. While Skinner did not adopt much of the rhetoric or don the outward appearances of the stereotypical black power advocate (e.g. the wearing of a dashiki or an Afro hairstyle), he did however put into practice many of its economic principles.

For example, the church, only fifteen years old, became a major stockholder in the black owned City National Bank of Newark. The rationale behind this acquisition was that if any of the church members needed a loan to start a business, they could use the church as a reference. In the early 1970s before malls were prominent in the United States, Skinner envisioned opening one-hundred businesses under one roof.

If members owned businesses, Skinner would advertise their services during church to help bolster sales. On some occasions, however, having reached his limit of patience with people who did not appear as if they wanted to get ahead in life with their businesses, he would lament stating: "You can't make a small mind great."

One of Skinner's visions was to build "Deliverance City" which was to be a large housing complex located in Newark, New Jersey. In the middle of the complex would be the five-thousand seats Deliverance Temple. There was even a scale model of Deliverance City in the vestibule of the Brooklyn church.

The mayor of Newark had even promised him land for this venture and the plans were in the works for this massive undertaking. It appeared as though the project was underway, when suddenly, the dream turned into disappointment when, without warning, the mayor reneged on his promise.

One of the goals of the Black Power Movement was economic independence. Skinner purchased land in Virginia to grow crops and sell at a discount price to his parishioners (Lockwood 1976). Skinner's otherworld view along with his desire to see his people get ahead, fueled his desire to become somewhat independent of this current world system.

Roy West, a local news commentator and community affairs specialist for radio station WPAT, visited the Deliverance Temple and made glowing compliments about Skinner and the Deliverance church on his broadcast. The following is a portion of his comments:

"[The Social Service] Department is as complete and much more organized than that of any municipality...it has sent literally hundreds of young people to college—young people who would not have had the opportunity were it not for the efforts and concern of the Deliverance Temple Church...."

Skinner was very aware of the unique circumstances he faced as a pastor of churches in the inner-city. Many of the youth were brought up in single parent homes with an absent father. The financial resources were limited and many of the adults had a limited education. Milmon Harrison, an African American sociologist, in his book, *Righteous Riches*, states:

"The religion and religious institutions of African slaves and their descendants in America have always had to be concerned with the material, social, political, and spiritual needs of their followers. To limit ministry to the spiritual realm was a luxury they could not afford...It was the role of the Black church...to take up the slack and meet the needs of the people." (Harrison 2007)

Skinner recognized that ministry was more than just spirituality. He understood that it would take more than a Sunday morning sermon to rescue many of the youths and adults from the plight of the inner-city. Some in the churches at large accused the devil for the ghettos and the economic predicament of those in the inner-cities. Skinner recognized the contribution of blatant racism and what Carter Woodson titled his book, *The Mis-Education of the Negro*, for much of the dilemma of African Americans in the inner-cities. Along with that, he also understood that salvation, along with "re-education," was vital if those in the inner-city were going to help stem the tide of their current condition.

Starting with re-education, Arturo was determined to raise the consciousness and standard of living of his parishioners. He first attempted to get us to look at ourselves differently than the stereotypical view, teaching us not to define ourselves by our surroundings or our ethnicity. He believed the re-education process started with self-esteem.

In some interviews with other former members of the church, I noticed a theme with many of them. One of the common compliments they had about Skinner was the self-esteem he built in them. Many times, he would build up their self-esteem and self-confidence by building them up before the church crowd of thousands. For example, if the person had an accomplishment, a talent or was an inspired minister, Skinner would speak of the person in glowing terms as though they were someone *very* accomplished.

Many of the youth had a limited exposure; all they knew was life in the inner-city. Every year Skinner took the pre and early teens to the circus at Madison Square Garden. No doubt, most of them would have never gone to the circus if it not for Skinner. Also in the summer, he provided young people with jobs.

I often heard Skinner say as he instructed his pastors, "If you help the poor, when they get on their feet they will help you." Skinner lived by that credo as many who could not pay their rent and others who could not buy proper clothing or food were subsidized with his personal money. Skinner often stated, "I don't want a single elderly person in my church to go to the supermarket to buy dog or cat food when they don't own a dog or cat."

Some people in the church owed their homes to the generosity of Arturo Skinner. In the book, *The Black Churches of Brooklyn,* Clarence Taylor relates one of the examples: "Samuel Gibson, although working as an unskilled laborer and as a caretaker of the church, managed to save some money and with a loan from the [Deliverance Center] church purchased a home in Bedford-Stuyvesant."

Pentecostals, marginalized by society, were touted as uneducated and unsophisticated. From the beginning of the Pentecostal movement, mostly blacks and poor whites attended the Azusa Street revival of 1906. Even during the sixties, Pentecostals were still, for the most part, marginalized by mainline church denominations. Says Synan:

"For six decades, (1901-60) Pentecostals were considered outside the pale of respectable Christianity in America and the world. The Pentecostals were noisy, and to many people, disorderly. On top of this, most Pentecostals were poor, underprivileged, uneducated..." (Synan 2003)

Arturo was attempting to change that image, at least for Deliverance, by exposing the youth and adults to things that they, under normal circumstances, would not be exposed. Every year there was a banquet at one of the exclusive hotels in New York or New Jersey. When the church went to places like the prestigious Waldorf Astoria, for example, to a formal banquet, we were not to act as though we were in church. While there was gospel singing and preaching, there was no speaking in tongues or dancing in the aisles. The affairs were always orderly; we lifted our hands in praise to God in a "dignified manner."

"Dad" Skinner

Skinner became a "father" to many of the youth. When he said he was your dad, it was not just rhetoric. He would become a mentor, many times setting-up trust funds for many of his "sons" and "daughters" and even for their children. For many of the youths, he paid for their weddings and for some he paid for their receptions, honeymoons, and even their college education. This was not solely for the children of his church, wherever he went across the country he would "adopt" children as his sons and daughters.

Arturo took to heart his role as dad, perhaps because he grew up in a single parent home with an absent father. This was my own experience with him in my early days of his ministry and he requested that I occasionally visit him in his office. On one of those visits when I was fifteen, he asked me about my family and specifically about my father. When I informed him that my father had died when I was six years old, he said to me in an assertive voice, "I'm your dad." His statement delighted me, as I knew he expected it would, so I smiled at him approvingly.

During Christmas, Skinner bought presents for many of his spiritual sons and daughters, allowing them to choose the gift. He asked me what I wanted for Christmas so I told him I wanted a Schofield Bible (a relatively pricey Bible). When I came to his office two weeks later, he smiled and afterward inquired, "What did you ask me for?" I noticed next to his desk was a box filled with presents and before I could respond, he had already taken out my present and began to remove the wrapping.

Skinner, at times, was as much a part of the lives of the youth of his church as their biological parents. An example of this is Van Dyke Freeman, one of those who grew up in Deliverance. In an interview he stated that when he misbehaved in school, his teacher, instead of calling his mother, would call Pastor Skinner.

For the Hispanic members who spoke little English, Skinner started a Spanish-speaking arm of the ministry. The services were held on Wednesday in one of the smaller sections of the Brooklyn church with Prince Marshall, one of the bi-lingual ministers in the church, conducting the services.

It is not my intention to create the impression that Skinner only ministered to blacks and those of the inner-city. His ministry reached all races and people from all lifestyles. However, he was located in the inner-city, so it only makes sense that his first commitment would be to those of his community.

As far as politics are concerned, it is not surprising that Skinner did not personally get involved politically. Skinner felt, as some black Pentecostals during that time, that politics are for the politicians. While he encouraged us to participate in the political process, vis-à-vis voting, he felt it unwise for preachers to be politicians. According to Skinner, ministry was a full-time undertaking and one might compromise his or her ministry obligations if he/she attempted to be a politician and a preacher.

MSG Crowd

CHAPTER SIX

Watchman, What of the Night?

*I have set watchmen on your walls, O Jerusalem. They shall
never hold their peace day or night.*

(Isaiah 62:6 NKJV)

In the black church, there is a style of preaching coined the "prophetic voice." The prophetic voice is a throwback to the prophets of the Bible who spoke as God directed them as they exposed the sins of a nation or a people, urging them to repent, calling them back to God. Scriptures, such as Isaiah 58:1 in which Isaiah was instructed by Yahweh to, "Cry aloud and spare not, lift up your voice like a trumpet in Zion, show my people their transgressions and the house of Jacob their sins." Other biblical texts are also used as justification for this genre of preaching. Obery Hendricks, a professor at New York Theological Seminary, states that, "Prophetic speech is characterized by an overwhelming sense of encounter with God and a message of moral and political judgment that a prophet feels divinely compelled to proclaim."

While not often stated, Skinner considered himself an apostle and a prophet. Skinner, in the tradition of the prophetic voice, railed against deceitful ministers, both black and white, which would prey upon unsuspecting persons in the church. During the decades of the 1950s and 1960s, there were some black ministers on their radio broadcasts promising money blessings and relief from "evil and bad luck" if the listener would purchase items such as "blest cabbage" along with other bizarre things. Many times, they instructed the listener to perform some rather peculiar ritual in order to receive blessings. One radio minister even claimed that God told him to call his particular blessing trinket "The Thing." The radio minister usually instructed his audience to meet him at a specific hotel at six o'clock in the morning [sic].

One of those ministers broadcasted on the same radio station as Skinner. On one occasion, the promo for this minister aired immediately following Skinner's broadcast. Concerned that someone would mistake him for the other minister; Skinner instructed the radio executives never to have this minister's promo after his broadcast. Along with accusing these ministers of fraudulent practices, Skinner wanted no affiliation with ministers that sold blessings.

For a time, Skinner refused to rent the Bedford Y.M.C.A. in Brooklyn for his meetings because another minister that charged a fee for people to enter, in addition to charging for blessings after they entered, also rented that particular Y.M.C.A. for his own meetings. Skinner did not want anyone to confuse him with this "crook" as he referred to him.

In some of the early days of his ministry, Skinner had no problem denouncing these ministers from his pulpit, along with sometimes mentioning their names. I recall one Saturday night during a service, this woman wanted prayer, claiming that she was vexed by an evil entity. She also claimed she had gone to a minister in Hampton, Virginia for help who charged her excessive fees, along with giving her some bizarre instructions while maintaining that she would be relieved of her vexation if she followed his instructions. Skinner asked the woman the minister's name. When she revealed his name, Skinner, speaking into the microphone, declared, "Doctor Cooz, (not necessarily the correct spelling) from Hampton, Virginia is a 'devil.'"

Skinner also disparaged some of the popular white ministers. This made some in the congregation uneasy, especially those who had been conditioned by the dominate society into believing that blacks were inferior to whites. This mind-set of "black inferiority" has led some blacks to believe that white ministers are somehow more anointed and more knowledgeable of the things of God than black ministers are. This resulted in many African Americans becoming vulnerable to unscrupulous white ministers. Consequently, many blacks gave an allegiance to the white evangelists even over and above their own churches and pastors.

Skinner respected many of the renowned evangelists such as Billy Graham and Oral Roberts, among others. However, his admiration did not extend to all of the well-known evangelists. I have heard Skinner state on a number of occasions that he questioned why so many of the white evangelists were accepted in the black community and not accepted in the white community. He concluded that if their gifts were so great, they should be accepted by their own people as well.

Skinner was suspect as to the motives of some of the popular evangelists. When considering the manner by which many of them conducted their crusades, he had sufficient grounds for his suspicions. The swindles of several of the evangelists ran the gambit from promises of miraculous healings and abundant wealth in exchange for a financial gift, to the threat of destruction by the hand of God if one did not give financially to their ministries.

Case in point, one well-known tent evangelist related a story to a predominately black audience, of a man who did not give to his ministry. The evangelist claimed that God [sic] burned down this man's trailer house and everything in it. This same evangelist equated not giving to his ministry as an *unpardonable* sin, via a story in which God *would not* forgive a man who, according to the evangelist, out of disobedience to God did not give an offering to his ministry.

These tactics infuriated Skinner. One time I was sitting near him in the pulpit when after he ended reprimanding the audience for being seduced by the claims of some of these unscrupulous ministers, he sat down and out of frustration banged his hand on the arm of his chair, mumbling some angry remarks. Many times he warned us not to attend the meetings of these evangelists, while not mentioning their names, it was obvious whom he was referring to because they were in town at that time, conducting a crusade. Arturo one time stated that he knew what was going on in the meetings of these evangelists because he sent his "spies" into the meetings.

A. A. Allen

Around 1966, some people I knew invited me to attend a crusade conducted by the renowned healing evangelist A. A. Allen, which he held at the Rockland Palace auditorium in Harlem, New York. In this particular service, Allen was raising money to buy a new tent for his crusades. Allen informed the audience that if they pledged a certain amount of money toward the purchase of the new tent, he would give them a swatch of his old tent, which he claimed was saturated with God's power. He also promised that it would bring miracles, healing, and blessings to those that possessed it.

The next Saturday when I returned to Deliverance, Skinner was cautioning his audience not to be duped into *buying* miracle prayer cloths from phony evangelists that came to town once a year. It was then that I became aware that Skinner numbered Allen among those deceitful ministers.

In 1970, when Allen died, the *Washington Post* affirmed that, according to the coroner's report, Allen's death was due to "Acute alcoholism and fatty infiltration of the liver." Skinner, I am sure was aware of the well-publicized arrest of Allen in 1955 on suspicion of drunken driving. Along with rumors of his excessive drinking, Skinner stated from his pulpit that he had known for years that Allen was a drunk. That statement made some in the congregation uncomfortable because many Pentecostals, both black and white, respected Allen as a man of God. Skinner, not deterred by criticisms of his diatribe of Allen and others of Allen's ilk, did not retract his statement.

"Where's the man with the blessing plan?"

Legal Dispute with Rev. Ike

One night at church, Skinner stood before the audience and in a mocking tone posed this rhetorical question: "Where's the man with the blessing plan?" This was in reference to a news report that Rev. Frederick Eikerenkoetter (a.k.a. Rev. Ike) was missing. Skinner had known Ike for a number of years. They met in the early days of their ministries before Ike revised his teaching to include the "Science of the Mind." Ike's unorthodox teaching had been denounced by Skinner along with the churches at large. Ike also espoused the "Blessing Plan," a prosperity teaching which Skinner condemned as well.

Skinner related to the audience that Ike had brought a lawsuit against him and now he was missing. He did not reveal the particulars of the lawsuit, but unconfirmed reports maintain that the lawsuit filed against Skinner was for copyright infringement, in which Skinner allegedly used a format from Ike's magazine without his permission. Sometime later Ike resurfaced. As far as my research has revealed, Ike dropped the lawsuit.

Skinner was not the only minister speaking against the abuses made by these ministers. Many of the other pastors and evangelists were very aware of the schemes some of the evangelists used to bilk people out of their finances. According to Harrell's book , *All Things Are Possible,* he states that, "All evangelists knew that some [evangelists] had succumbed to the evil triumvirate, 'women, money, and popularity.'" In addition, quoting Don Basham, a respected neo-Pentecostal, Harrell writes, "We have this problem of 'false ministers' who were guilty of dishonesty, immorality, and deception" (Harrell 1978). Many other pastors spoke of these abuses among themselves. Skinner, in contrast, spoke against these "predatory practices" publically. As a result he was criticized for speaking out against these ministers.

Prosperity/Word of Faith Theology

Presently preachers, both black and white, who appear on much of the electronic media, will most likely not threaten their congregations with disaster if they do not give to their ministries. What you do hear, on the other hand, by those that advocate a "prosperity gospel" is the promise that, in exchange for a financial donation, God will make the donor financially wealthy. Juxtaposed to this, the "hyper-faith" minister proposes that the Christian can exercise "The God kind of faith," i.e. the same kind of faith that God uses [sic].

There were questions posed to me stating if Arturo Skinner was alive today, what would most likely be his reaction to the hyper-faith (a.k.a. Word of Faith) message in this current era of the mega-church phenomenon? In addition, what would possibly be his response to the prosperity gospel that has engaged so many in Pentecostal and charismatic churches?

Obviously, I can only speculate on his response based on my knowledge of past responses he gave on related topics. For example, his opposition to the emphasis on faith compared to how he would react to the modern hyper-faith message. As mentioned earlier, he contested the label "faith healer" because he reasoned that the title "faith healer" put the emphasis upon faith and not God. In addition, Skinner's negative reaction to Ike's blessing plan may well be comparable to his response to the present day prosperity gospel.

Nonetheless, Skinner promoted the book, *In His Presence* by E.W. Kenyon. This was before the so-called Word of Faith Movement was as prevalent as it is today and there are numerous studies and books written on this sect of the church. One such work is, D.R. McConnell's *A Different Gospel*, written in 1988. McConnell's well-documented book revealed that E.W. Kenyon is the originator of the modern Word of Faith theology (McConnell 1988).

Apparently, Skinner adhered to some aspects of the hyper-faith message in that he promoted Kenyon's book and that some of Word of Faith theology and the theology of those of the healing revival overlap. Based on the comparisons mentioned above, along with other Word of Faith teachings; for instance, the belief that Christians are little gods, and that Jesus took into His spirit the nature of Satan; died spiritually while on the Cross and consequently had to be born again, I conclude that Skinner would have taken exception to most of the contemporary hyper-faith message. Especially one of its core beliefs that espouse that even God uses faith. Furthermore, I conclude that Skinner would strongly object to the vast *emphasis* placed upon financial blessings, which is characteristic of the modern-day prosperity gospel. I further suggest that if Skinner perceived that the pastors of the modern mega-churches were building their mega-ministries by deifying faith and using prosperity as a lure to attract crowds, he would protest in the strongest terms and counsel those ministers to revise their teachings.

In addition, I do not believe that Skinner would be comfortable in the current climate of preachers flaunting their affluence before the world. While Skinner did live well, he did not live "too far" above his congregation.

Admonishing the Church

The prophetic voice was not limited to admonishing unscrupulous ministers and their practices. As mentioned earlier, Pentecostals believe that the Christians should live a sanctified life by separating themselves from the evil ways of the world. There were those in the congregation who willfully sinned, not living up to the Pentecostal standard of holiness. Skinner, many times, admonished the wayward Christian during a sermon or in some cases in private. The reproofs, known as "chastening," were remedial in their design so that the Christian would not be "condemned with the world."

Many Holiness pioneers of the early 20th century adopted the Wesleyan-perfectionist view of sanctification. Wesley's view, as noted by Ithiel Clemmons in his work *Bishop C.H. Mason and the Roots of the Church of God in Christ*, states, "Wesley consistently defines sin as the violation of known laws of God—which is to say, voluntary and deliberate." That is, by not sinning *deliberately*, the Christian can live sinless. Skinner did not subscribe to this restricted definition of sin, but believed that not all sins are intentional; one may sin and not be aware of the sin, therefore making it impossible to live sinless.

According to Skinner, he would never compromise what he considered the truth, even if it cost him members, money or friends. On one occasion, Skinner preached a message entitled, "The Reproach of Being Called an Apostle." In this sermon, he typifies the ostracism and persecution one has to endure because of their calling. Moreover, in his "prophetic role," he thought it his obligation to speak the truth without compromise or consideration of to whom he spoke the truth. Many times it cost him friends and support, however he believed if one had the call of God, there was a price one must pay and a standard one must not compromise.

Rev. Ralph Nichol

**Rare Photo Apostle Skinner. His brother Buck
Oakland, Calif., Celebrating Buck's birthday**

Apostle Skinner

Mother Corinne Austin
Evangelist Supervisor

Missionary Olga Small

Mother Mary Amarty

Mother Emmaline Moe

Mother Carrie Black
1st Lady of Deliverance

Sister Louise Durant,
Cousin

Mother Maude Heywood,
Aunt

PIONEERING WOMEN

IN

DELIVERANCE

MOVEMENT

Mother Ethel Askew

94

Chapter Seven

We've Got to Do it Now

*I'm laying aside every weight that I might be able to run. I
don't want to walk now; I want to run this race.*
> —Arturo Skinner, "We've Got to Do It Now"

Typically, after a Saturday service Skinner walked down the middle aisle with his entourage of junior pastors and his security following. I often stood in the back of the church when he exited the sanctuary to his office. He regularly looked at me and nodded his head as he walked by acknowledging my presence; and I reciprocated with a nod. The last time I saw him, he was exiting the sanctuary after a Saturday service and nodded to me as usual, however I noticed he looked extremely worn. I dismissed it by concluding that perhaps he was just exhausted. I did not realize that that would be the last nod I would receive from Apostle Skinner.

The next Saturday, I did not attend church, and Skinner was also missing from church. I immediately sensed that something was amiss as he would not be absent from church unless on vacation or on a crusade out of town. He also missed the Sunday and Tuesday night services. The explanation given to the church was that Skinner had gone to the mountains to shut-in and pray. Only a select few knew that he was in his apartment, his life fading away.

In Skinner's absence, two of the ministers of the church, James (Jimmy) Everett, son of Doretha Everett and Ralph Nichol were assigned the task of preaching on Saturdays and Sundays. The

Saturday service was the radio broadcast and whoever preached the broadcast would be heard around the world. Jimmie Gilliard, the radio director, decided that Nichol would be best suited for that coveted position.

"For to me, to live is Christ and to die is gain" —Apostle Paul, Philippians 1:21

Skinner had been sick for years yet he prayed for the sick by the thousands weekly. Sometime earlier, according to his valet, the seriousness of Skinner's illness became apparent when he noticed that one of his legs had turned black. His valet, being shocked by what he observed exclaimed, "Pastor Skinner what's that?!" Skinner responding nonchalantly said, "I don't know."

Dennis Tucker, business manager and nephew of Skinner, in a communiqué to me recalled one ominous Tuesday prior to Skinner's death:

"It was Tuesday night prayer service. Very rarely had I attended, but I decided to on this night. Pastor Skinner had been ill and losing strength. As I walked around for the offering and prayer, Pastor Skinner was sitting in a chair with the offering table in front of him. I reached out, left my offering and touched his hand."

"Shortly after that Tuesday night prayer service, I received a phone call early in the morning, around 1:00AM from [his valet] Alfred Simmons. He was calling because Pastor Skinner's condition had worsened to the point Brother Simmons wanted to take him to the hospital. He called because he needed consent from a relative."

In an interview with Simmons, I informed him of Tucker's claim. Simmons stated that, "Pastor Skinner refused to go to the hospital." Skinner did not denounce doctors, yet still when he was sick unto death, he did not seek medical attention. I suppose that he held himself to what he believed to be a high standard of faith by not seeking medical attention. On March 20th, Skinner slipped into a coma and was taken to New York Hospital.

Arturo Alfred Skinner was pronounced dead at New York Hospital on Thursday March 20, 1975 at 2:45 p.m. I remember that Thursday when I returned from work and my mother called me. I answered the phone and in jest asked who died, not expecting to hear that someone had actually died. She then answered me directly, "Arturo Skinner." She remained silent for a second or two waiting on my response. I broke the silence stating that I was going to make some phone calls to validate her information.

After the account of his death had spread, as one would imagine, ministers and laypeople alike expressed shock at the news of his sudden passing. Two noteworthy mentions are Bishop Roy E. Brown, a prominent Brooklyn pastor who dedicated part of his popular radio broadcast speaking on the work and ministry of Arturo Skinner. In addition, Skinner's father in the gospel, Bishop Roderick R. Caesar Sr., according to his son, stated that his father publically expressed sadness at Skinner's passing with glowing remarks, commenting that his death was a great loss to the body of Christ.

No one can dispute that for the most part the persona of Arturo Skinner attracted the crowds, and now he was dead. If the church was to continue on its course and maintain its recognition, it would have to appoint another minister with the skill, charisma, experience, and admiration of the people as Arturo Skinner.

Adding to the devastating loss of a beloved leader, Skinner had not publicly chosen anyone to replace him in the event of his demise. On the other hand, I suppose that he did not anticipate that his life would end so unexpectedly at the age of only fifty years old. As far as I have uncovered, there were no written instructions left by Skinner on how things should continue in the event of his death. Then again, as organized and practical as he was, it does not seem feasible that he did not have anything written on how the church should function if he were to pass on.

Daisy Moose, one of the mothers of the church, was one of those attending to Skinner during his illness. Unfortunately, she expired before I could interview her. In an interview with her daughter, Barbara Moose-Jacobs, who alleges that during one of those visits to Skinner's home, he revealed to her mother who he desired to pastor the church in the event of his death. According to Jacobs, Skinner's choice for his successor was his crusade manager Jimmy Everett. While Jacobs' assertion is plausible, I have not found anyone that could corroborate this claim.

According to one inside source, Skinner started receiving invitations to minister overseas. His plans, according to my source, were to appoint seventy elders to take charge of the ministry while he spent time ministering abroad. How far these plans had developed in respect to implementation is not known.

All the same, Deliverance was a fellowship of churches and not an organization. As a result, the other apostles had no legal authority in determining who would preside over the fellowship or pastor the church. To add to this, there was no board of directors in control of the fellowship, so the responsibility of choosing a new leader fell into the hands of the Board of Trustees. With little to no outside counsel, the Trustee Board being inexperienced in these matters, appointed Ralph Nichol, a convert of about seven years, as acting pastor. Although Nichol was a relatively new convert, he rose quickly through the ranks, becoming a popular preacher within the church. His fiery brand of preaching earned him high approval from Skinner and many of the church members.

A short time later, the board, realizing they made a hasty decision, attempted to depose Nichol. By this time, however, Nichol had gained the support of a major portion of the congregation along with the approval of Alfred Simmons and Billy Wooten, two influential and outspoken members in the church. After no small feud between the Board of Trustees and the greater part of the congregation, the congregation forced the leadership of the board out. Subsequent to the ousting of the trustee leadership, the congregation, being in a state of flux and vulnerable, at the prompting of Simmons, voted to expand Nichol's authority to include Overseer of the entire Deliverance fellowship. Nichol, however, was inexperienced as a pastor and untested as a leader. These deficiencies would prove devastating to his administration.

Shortly after his appointment, several of the ministers of the church started their own ministries, attracting many of the church members. Along with that, Apostle Johnnie Washington, the pastor of The Tabernacle of Prayer in Jamaica, New York, whose church services were similar to that of Skinner's, attracted a number of the influential members. To make matters worse, among the few pastors that remained in the fellowship, several of them joined other fellowships and organizations taking along with them their congregations. Furthermore, a number of the remaining congregates were dismissed by Nichol while others became disillusioned with his administration and left for other assemblies.

All of this proved overwhelming for the young novice pastor and as a result the membership dwindled. There were no more buses crowding the streets, the sea of choir members dressed in black and white with their red "Christ is the Answer" buttons were all but gone. By the late 1980s, a once thriving church had become a dismal replica of its former self. At the time of this writing, Nichol is still the pastor of the Temple in Newark. Sadly however, Nichol sold the Brooklyn church and the new owners demolished the building.

I was asked which one of the sons of the church I thought could pastor the church after Pastor Skinner's death and still keep some semblance of its former glory. I did a survey of some of the earlier members of the church and overwhelmingly the name of Harold J. Benjamin, the former pastor of the Pennsylvania Deliverance Center, was brought-up. However, as mentioned earlier, Benjamin left the organization in 1969 under a storm of controversy after a dispute with Skinner.

Deliverance Ministries since Skinner

The evangelical church's obsession with demons has increased in recent years. This is evident by the rise of numerous so-called deliverance ministries within evangelicalism, along with a plethora of books, CDs, and DVDs on the subject of spiritual warfare.

I will not address the accuracy or inaccuracy of these "deliverance ministries," just their existence. One of the many popular works on spiritual warfare is Frank Peretti's 1986 novel, *This Present Darkness*. Once a relatively unknown author, his book has sold multitudes of copies and has become a "must read" for many evangelical Christians.

Deliverance ministries vary in their "revelation" of the demonic sphere. Many claim that it is possible for Christians to become *demonized*. Others state that "generational curses" are the cause for many people's dilemmas.

Some even claim that the Christian should be cautious about what one confesses to God in one's prayers, especially some weakness about one's self. The reason being is that demons are possibly listening to the confession, and with that information gains an advantage, thereby making the Christian vulnerable to demonic attacks. Still others teach that Christians can even cast demons out of themselves [sic].

Also, without engaging in spiritual warfare, some teach that the Christian will not be as successful in evangelizing. In a practice known as "spiritual mapping" the Christian studies the background of the region in which he/she intends to evangelize in order to determine which "territorial spirit (demon)" is assigned to that region. Armed with that information, the Christian confronts the demon(s) and "binds" them thereby breaking strongholds over the region making a way for successful evangelization.

A few years after Skinner's death, I visited one of the contemporary "deliverance" churches. In this particular church all the Christians in the service in need of deliverance from demonic possession were being ministered to by those with buttons that read "demon chaser." All around me were people with plastic buckets in which they were coughing into and drinking water. I asked the person that invited me the purpose of drinking water. She told me that that is the "witness of the water." When I asked her to elaborate, she could not give a satisfactory explanation, so I did not press the issue.

According to the pastor of the church, during these "deliverance sessions" demons left the Christians' bodies by way of a cough or a yawn [sic]. Those people who did not receive their deliverance before the close of the service were instructed by the pastor to "box-up" the demon until next service. I believe I am safe in stating that Skinner would have never approved of this exhibition or explanation of deliverance.

On A Personal Note

Some people I have spoken to in doing research for this book, expressed to me how they desired to have things as they were when Arturo Skinner was alive. Possibly these people have failed to consider that just may not be on God's agenda. In the book of Acts, the church was gathered at Jerusalem rejoicing and basking in the afterglow of the infilling of the Spirit. However, that was not the will of God for *all* of the church to remain at Jerusalem. Some of the disciples were to spread across the nations and preach the gospel.

For the reader's consideration, perhaps Deliverance was just a *move* of God and those that bask in its feel-good factor are turning it into a *monument*. Moreover, perhaps God wanted those people affected by Skinner's ministry not to remain at "Jerusalem" but to spread throughout the land and do ministry. I am not suggesting that we forget what we have witnessed, but not to lay stakes there. Many persons affected by Arturo Skinner's ministry that were menaces to society are now preaching the gospel and carrying on the work of the gospel across this nation and around the world. I believe Pastor Skinner did indeed accomplish the purpose of God by bringing into the kingdom people who would not have been there otherwise.

Call My Name and I Will Live Forever

The approach of Arturo Skinner toward ministry can be summed up in the title of one of his last sermons entitled, "We've Got To Do it Now." This sermon, in my view, is part of the legacy that he left to those who were influenced by his ministry. His urgency to "Get the job done," as he phrased it, stimulated his passion and is why he worked so tirelessly to *"Do it NOW!"* Perhaps no one characterized this sermon better than Alfred Simmons did when he penned the lyrics:

"All that's left is time to live for Jesus, no more time to walk in our own way. All that's left is time to live for Jesus; life is just too short to waste away." *All that's left is Time to Live for Jesus."* Words and music by Alfred Simmons

Skinner routinely closed his letters with the salutation, *"Yours because of Calvary."* I believe that was his way of recognizing that it was because of the Cross of Calvary everything that was accomplished in his life was brought about. As he often stated in his prayer prior to his sermons "[God] hide me behind the Cross of Calvary."

The following is a verse of a song which seems most befitting to the consummation of this book and epitomizes Skinner's unique salutation:

"Just let me live my life, and let it be pleasing Lord to thee and if I should gain any praise let it go to Calvary." *My Tribute (To God be the Glory)*. Words and music by Andrae Crouch.

There is an African saying that states, "Call my name and I will live forever." That is, if you speak of a loved one who has passed, you pay homage to that person and the memory never dies. For that reason, I give glory to God for the grace He bestowed upon the ministry and life of Apostle Arturo Skinner.

Since his death, his influence has spawned many imitators from among the sons and daughters of his ministry, as some of them, and even those not of Deliverance, have assumed the title "apostle." I believe the best way to pay tribute to him is to take his example of dedication and *passionately* do what the Lord has called the individual to do, to the glory and honor of the Lord Jesus Christ.

Subway Advertisement

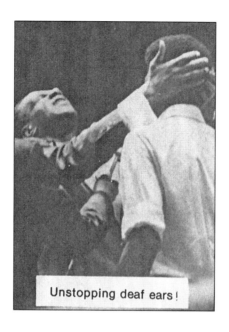

Unstopping deaf ears!

The Watson Family—LtoR Grace, Barbara, Mother, Violet Watson, Judge James Watson, Jr.

The Watsons

Apostle Skinner

Bibliography

Burgess, Stanley M. and McGee, Gary B. eds.: Alexander, Patrick H. associate ed. *Dictionary of Pentecostal and Charismatic Movements*. Grand Rapids, MI.: Zondervan Publishing House, 1996.

Clemmons, Ithiel C. *Bishop C.H. Mason and the Roots of the Church of God in Christ: Centennial Edition*. Bakersfield, CA. Pnuema Life Publishing, 1996.

Cox, Harvey. *Fire from Heaven: The Rise of Pentecostal Spirituality and the Reshaping of Religion in the 21st Century*. New York and Cambridge, MA: Da Capo Press, 2001.

Deliverance Bible Institute Outreach Journal, 1967.

Deliverance Evangelistic Centers 7th Anniversary Journal, 1965.

Deliverance First Women's Day Service Journal, September, 1959.

Deliverance Voice, 4 no.4, April, 1970.

Deliverance Voice 5 no.5, May, 1971.

Deliverance Voice, 6 no.5, September-October, 1972.

Deliverance Voice, 9 no.3, September-October, 1975.

Deliverance Yours Because of Calvary Journal, 1969.

Harrell, David E. *All Things are Possible: The Healing and Charismatic Revival in Modern America:* Bloomington & London: Indiana University Press, 1975.

Harrison, Milmon F. *Righteous Riches: The Word of Faith Movement in Contemporary African American Religion:* New York, NY: Oxford University Press Inc., 2005.

Lincoln, C. Eric and Mamiya, Lawrence H. *The Black Church in the American Experience*: Durham, N.C.: Duke University Press,

1998.

Lockwood, Lelia M. *When I Met the Master*. New York, N.Y.: Park Publishing Company, 1976.

McConnell, Dan R. *A Different Gospel: Updated Edition*. Peabody, Mass.: Hendrickson Publishers Inc., 1995.

Murphy, Larry G. Melton, Gordon and Ward, Gary L. eds. *Encyclopedia of African American Religions*. New York and London: Garland Publishing, 1993.

Salley, Columbus and Behm, Ronald text copyright *Your God Is Too White: An Illustrated Documentary of Christianity and Race in America*. Inter Varsity Press, USA *Ilustrated edition, 1973*. Lion Publishing Berkhamsted, Herts, 1970.

Skinner, Arturo. *9 Gifts of the Spirit*. Newark, N. J. Deliverance Publishing House, 1975.

_____, "When I Met the Master" Tape: Sermon (circa. 1973) Chicago, Ill.

Synan, Vinson 1971.: *The Holiness Pentecostal Movement in the United States*. Grand Rapids MI. William B. Eerdmans Publishing Company

The Century of the Holy Spirit: 100 Years of Pentecostal and Charismatic Renewal 1901-2001 Nashville, Tenn. Thomas Nelson Inc., 2001.

Taylor, Clarence. 1994. *The Black Churches of Brooklyn*: New York Chester, West Sussex:. Columbia University Press.

Wilmore, Gayraud S. *Black Religion and Black Radicalism: An Interpretation of the Religious History of African Americans*: Maryknoll, N Y.: Orbis Books, 1998.

About the Author

James Blocker is the pastor and founder of the Maranatha Tabernacle located in Queens, New York. As an itinerate evangelist he has traveled extensively across the United States. Pastor Blocker also serves as an Overseer of the *New Life Fellowship of Churches* headquartered in Topeka, KS.

Pastor Blocker did his undergraduate studies at College of New Rochelle where he received his B.A. degree. He also studied at the United Christian College toward a Doctor of Sacred Theology degree.

At fifteen years old, he was introduced to Apostle Arturo Skinner. For the next ten years he closely followed Apostle Skinner and his ministry, attending crusades and, on occasion, traveling with him on crusades out of town.

Pastor Blocker is the husband of Wandra who assists him in ministry. They have three children and two grandsons.

This is Pastor Blocker's second book. His first book *The War Against the Church* is on the subject of spiritual warfare. This book can be purchased on Amazon.com; Barnes and Noble.com; Googlebooks.com, and Xulonpress.com.; or by contacting the author by writing to: James Blocker P.O. Box 340828 Jamaica, New York 11434-0828 Dept. A.

CPSIA information can be obtained at www.ICGtesting.com
Printed in the USA
BVOW011926120113

310428BV00006B/110/P